CW00446990

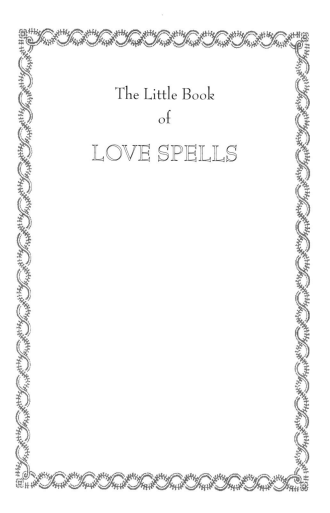

The Little Book

of

LOVE SPELLS

For all lovers, at all times,
and in all places . . .

The Little Book

of

LOVE
SPELLS

Edited by

Joules Taylor

p

This is a Parragon Book
This edition published in 2000

Parragon
Queen Street House
4 Queen Street
Bath BA1 1HE, UK

Produced by Magpie Books, an imprint of
Constable & Robinson Ltd, London

Copyright © Parragon 1999

ISBN 0-75253-926-4

A copy of the British Library Cataloguing-in-
Publication Data is available from the British Library

Printed and bound in China

Contents

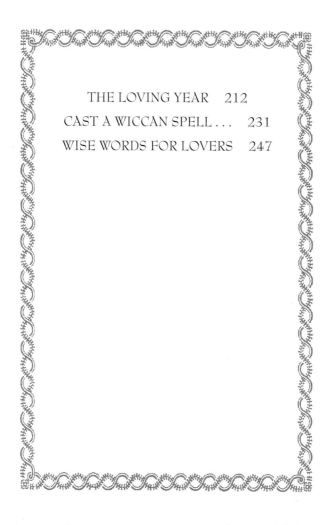

Introduction

So much has been written about love, through the ages. It's the most mysterious of all feelings, difficult to understand, impossible to control, at the same time the most fragile and powerful of emotions. From the warm, tender bond between parent and child, to the strong, staunch and mellow love of couples who have spent their lives together, we can't live without it!

But sometimes things don't go quite according to plan: occasionally a little help — a little magic — is needed to smooth the way and create happiness where there was sorrow. That's where this book may help.

Magic is nothing more, or less, than making

things happen — purely through the power of your will. Some people are able to do this within themselves, while others need an external object — a talisman or amulet — as a focus. Some prefer a spoken charm, or the emotional satisfaction of a full ritual designed to enhance romantic potential. You will find all of this and more in this book, and we wish you good luck in your search for love and happiness. However, it is wise to remember the greatest charm of all — to BE charming!

Caveat
We cannot guarantee the infallibility of any of the spells, charms or talismans in these pages.

THE GODS OF LOVE . . .
AND HOW TO
PETITION THEM!

~❧~

Throughout history, and in every culture in the world, there have been deities dedicated to love in all its various forms. From conjugal bliss to orgiastic fervor, from shy mutual attraction to serious flirtation, somewhere there is a god or goddess who fits the bill.

There are a number of ways of petitioning the deities – offerings of incense, flowers, fruit or other material objects, sacrifice (usually of something small and personal, like a lock of hair, a drop of blood, or a favorite item of clothing), or by dedicating oneself to their service for a length of time. By far the easiest method, however, is by prayer. Prayers are, quite simply, spells spoken or thought to focus the mind and will on a desired goal, and to request the assistance of the powers-that-be in the achieving of that goal.

The following pages detail some of the better known love deities and give examples of the objects and prayers associated with them. You might find that one or more of these lovely gods and goddesses appeal deeply to you and your desires: in which case, try asking them for their aid in your romantic life! As long as you don't become obsessed (something to be avoided at all costs, in all things) you might find yourself pleasantly surprised . . .

ISIS AND OSIRIS

~

Osiris – "the Good One" – and his wise and just wife Isis are reputed to have brought civilization to the then-savage land of Egypt. Between them they taught agricultural practices, laid down the precepts for religious observances, and created the first musical instruments. Osiris loathed violence: it was his compassion and sweetness of character that brought him success in all he attempted – his enemies were simply disarmed by the gentle strength of his personality . . .

While her husband was away charming his enemies, Isis governed Egypt to perfection. She embodied fertility, wisdom and female magic, and it was she who sought out and restored Osiris' body to life after his jealous brother Set had killed him.

Isis and Osiris symbolize perfected married happiness: they are equals in power and ability, devoted to each other and wise in their care of their "children." Those wishing for such qualities in their own relationships might like to address a simple prayer to the pair at sunrise and sunset:

"Wise Isis, gentle Osiris, may your love and devotion echo in my love and life."

Corn, grapes and acacia are special to Osiris, while the lotus, figs, myrrh, and dates are appropriate for Isis: share the fruits as a love feast to confirm your love, and wear the Ankh, the ancient symbol of Life, to keep it fresh and strong.

JUPITER AND JUNO

~

Although originally an agricultural deity (responsible for the weather and the sunlight that helped the crops to grow), Jupiter rapidly became seen as the great protector: he symbolized justice and honor, and was the guardian of the young. He was very much a patriarch, sometimes heavy-handed, but usually tempering discipline with wisdom.

Juno was the protectress of women, especially mothers and those in labor, and may be visualized as a guiding light, helping the new baby in its vital journey from the womb. She was the matriarch, the equal of her husband. As a goddess of childbirth, Juno's help was invoked by those having difficulty conceiving children.

Together, Jupiter and Juno symbolize wise parenthood and protection, especially for those just embarking on raising a family.

Nutmeg, cloves, almonds and olives are Jupiter's plants. The iris, lily and verbena are Juno's plants, and her special attribute is the peacock's tail feather (the eyes symbolize her constant watchfulness over her children). The first of March is Juno's particular day: while success can't, of course, be guaranteed, childless couples longing for children might like to dedicate this time to a special attempt. Share some olives or almonds, and address a small respectful prayer to the pair – the wording should be of your own devising. If you can burn some myrrh incense (light a charcoal tablet in an ashtray and sprinkle some grains on it once it's glowing) so much the better.

ZEUS AND HERA

~

This pair is included here more as a way of warding off unwanted behavior rather than encouraging it!

Zeus is renowned for his infidelities. His marriage to Hera did not stop his philandering, and he stopped at nothing – literally – in his lust for physical fulfillment. Hera, on the other hand, was entirely faithful to her husband. She was also very jealous of Zeus' amours, and quite capable of visiting terrible punishments on the women involved – even though they were usually completely blameless!

Zeus symbolizes the archetypal chauvinist, a type to be avoided (unless you're a masochist). Hera symbolizes both the vindictive, embittered wronged wife and the proud, virtuous, unattainable beauty –

either can cause a great deal of heartbreak.

Oranges, peppermint and the poplar tree are Zeus' plants. If you are troubled by an unwanted attraction to a modern-day Zeus, take an orange, some peppermint leaves and a handful of cloves. Pin the mint leaves to the orange with the cloves, saying, as each clove pierces the skin:

"With this act I drive you, [name], from my mind and my heart. Begone and trouble me no more."

Leave the charm somewhere dry, so that you can watch it wrinkle and harden, feeling your attraction to the person die with it. (If you are actually *in* a relationship with such a person, it might be better to seek professional help . . .)

To ward off an attraction to someone you know is prone to jealousy and will make your life miserable, tie five knots in a long, supple willow twig and either bury it or throw it into fast-running water, saying:

16

"I bind this affection with Hera's knots and send it far from me."

If, however, you are attracted to the beautiful but chaste variety – good luck! Be certain you can stay faithful yourself before trying to win your beloved. (For charms and spells for fidelity, see the appropriate sections in this book!)

APHRODITE

~

Aphrodite was the goddess of love – ALL love, from the noblest idealized romance to simple unbridled lust: her different names reflect the different kinds of love. Prayers to her must come from the heart, and be phrased in your own words.

So, for a pure love, address your prayers to Aphrodite Urania, and carry or wear chrysoprase or dioptase.

Aphrodite Genetrix protects married love and the family, and is the patroness of those wishing for a spouse, or wanting to renew the sparkle in their marriage. Jade is the luckiest stone for this aspect.

Aphrodite Nymphia listens to the appeals of those who are young and just starting out on their life-long journey into love and romance. Malachite and amazonite are most beneficial, either worn or carried.

Address petitions to Aphrodite Pandemos if all you're after is a wild time! Wear peridot or bloodstone to help give you the energy to keep going until dawn . . .

To bring love into a lonely life, or to enhance the relationship you already have, wear emeralds (Aphrodite's special gem); prepare a meal that includes apricots, strawberries and cinnamon; and ensure you have at least one red rose on the table. If you are able to burn some sandalwood incense, the spell will be enhanced. As you eat, concentrate on opening your mind and heart to loving influences – and be sure to clean and carry the apricot stone with you, for luck.

EROS

~

Treat Eros with care – he is capricious and quite capable of causing heartache!

Eros was the son of Aphrodite – a beautiful, sometimes gracious, sometimes malicious child who took great pleasure in torturing men with the fires of unrequited love. If you find yourself so afflicted, you might be able to deflect the worst of your suffering by taking bay leaves, writing the initial letter of your unattainable beloved's name on them, and burning them: this may act to remove the curse.

Alternatively, you could try appealing to Eros' mother: Aphrodite might be persuaded to reverse the situation – or even intervene to bring your love to fruition, especially if you've shown her devotion in the past!

ODIN AND FRIGG

~

Odin was the granter of heroism and victory in battle, and he also decreed the fates of humans. His wife, Frigg, protected marriages and intimate relationships and made them fruitful: she was the equal of her husband in wisdom and foresight. However, neither of them was particularly faithful, making them ideal for those couples who, although happy together, prefer an "open" relationship, taking others as lovers from time to time.

It is very important that both parties agree whole-heartedly to this state of affairs (and it's wise to think at least twice if you have children). If this is the case, to ensure that things run smoothly, keep acorns and mistletoe in the house. (The oak tree is Odin's plant, while mistletoe is special to both Odin and Frigg – to live near an oak on which mistletoe is growing would be the ideal situation, but since this is fairly unlikely, their seeds will suffice.) Carved bowls of ash or elm wood are also lucky: keep nuts, especially hazelnuts, in them to help you make wise choices. (You could also keep your spare change in them for financial luck.)

THE CELTS

~

Unlike many of their neighbors, the Celtic peoples did not have a rigidly defined pantheon, and because they were so widespread, the Celts in different countries often had different names and slightly different functions for their deities. Originally, there were no deities specifically responsible for love or romance, but over time some have come to be viewed as symbolizing aspects of the emotional side of life . . .

Generally speaking, Celtic deities may be most effectively invoked at springs and wells, and it's always wise to leave a small token of thanks — for example a coin, preferably silver — in the water (the Celts were the originators of the wishing well).

One thing to remember when considering Celtic deities is that in Celtic society, at least in its early days, women were accorded equal rank with men. Inheritance was through the mother, and women fought in battle alongside men (and sometimes with even more ferocity!) If you are a woman seeking a strong, powerful deity to help you cope with the stresses of modern life and love, one of the following might be right for you!

MORRIGAN

~

The warrior goddess. Her birds are the crow and raven, the carrion birds who feed on the dead at the field of battle, and her color is black.

Morrigan is implacable in action, and has an understanding of the natural order of life – that things are born, die and are reborn. While always ready to do battle, she is never vindictive, and has a keen sense of justice.

Morrigan is the ideal deity to call on if you are in a difficult, stressful relationship and want out. Carry a black stone as a talisman and ask to borrow her strength before confronting the source of the friction: be sure to finish it decisively and with no backward glances.

ANGUS

~

Angus was the son of the Dagda, originally the principal fertility god. His status as a love deity is fairly recent.

His function seems mainly to bring fond affection and light-heartedness into relationships. If you are finding things a little heavy going – perhaps with a partner who is under stress at work – gather some golden colored flowers and a couple of citrines, dedicate them to Angus and ask him to brighten the atmosphere between you.

If possible, buy some mead (liquor made with honey) and share a glassful before retiring each night, to foster loving feelings and bring pleasant dreams . . .

THE EARTH GODDESS

∾

A "triple goddess," often referred to as Bride or Bridget. She represented the fertile, nourishing aspect of the earth as well as the three stages of female life (maiden, mature woman and mother, post-menopausal).

To invoke her stability and endurance when faced with a difficult task (like saying "it's over" to a clinging lover you have outgrown but still feel affection for), bury, underneath a pine or oak tree, a small personal sacrifice (a lock of hair or drop of blood, for example) while mentally asking to be granted the strength to perform the task without harming anyone.

CERNUNNOS

~

The Lord of the Dance, also called the horned god; Cernunnos symbolizes male fertility. He is the protector of wild animals, and with the Earth Goddess embodies wholeness and creative power.

His power may be invoked for male complaints — impotence or male infertility, for example (though obviously also get medical advice!) Take a rock crystal wand — the size doesn't matter as long as it is longer than it is broad — to a solitary oak tree. Lean against the trunk, holding the crystal with both hands: close your eyes and imagine yourself being filled with energy drawn from the tree, the sun, the air, the earth itself. Focus this energy into the crystal, and keep the stone with you at all times.

SHIVA AND SHAKTI

~

Shiva and Shakti symbolize joy and enlight-
enment. Shiva is the dancing god — he
destroys illusions, thus allowing the individual to fully participate in and enjoy the
game of life (literally "dancing for joy"). He
embodies the harmonious union of oppo-
sites within the whole, enabling those who
understand his nature to see and love themselves for what they are — and to forgive
themselves for what they may see as their
faults and flaws.

Shakti is his female counterpart, without
whom he is incomplete; she embodies
beauty, pleasure and the happiness that
comes with self-acceptance. Her energy is
playful and seductive.

Both are invoked through dance: not
formal dancing, but the dance that comes

from within and expresses inner joy and freedom. Some people may find this difficult to start with, since it involves a genuine opening of the self to the gaze of another, and even if that one is the beloved, there is often a reticence and sense of vulnerability if you have not tried it before. Try dancing by yourself until you feel comfortable with the idea — imagine yourself expressing your love for your partner in your movements. After a while you can dance for each other, and then *with* each other, using the movements to weave a love-spell between and around you.

Poppy and jasmine (the latter can be bought as a fragrancer oil and used to scent the air while you dance) are special to Shakti, while Shiva's plants are the banyan tree and the marjoram herb.

KUAN-YIN

～

The Chinese goddess of mercy and compassion. While not exactly a love deity, her gentleness and healing abilities make this goddess the perfect patron for all those who have been hurt, humiliated or abandoned in love.

Find a solitary place, preferably near a pool – if it contains water lilies, Kuan-yin's plant, so much the better. Sit quietly and calm your mind, then mentally ask her to listen while you explain what ails your spirit. She is renowned for her patience, and will let you talk through your problems without interruption. Let her kindness and sympathy fill your mind and calm your emotions: the tranquillity of the place will soothe your spirit and allow you to leave with a renewed sense of self-worth.

Before you go, be sure to thank Kuan-yin for her solace. And remember that a small donation to a charity of your choice (especially one of the children's charities) will reinforce the effect and ensure her continued good wishes!

HYMN TO ISHTAR

～

(Ishtar is the Assyro-Babylonian goddess of
love and war. She is not a deity to be invoked
lightly, as she can be malicious if scorned or
forgotten, but in times of extreme need her
great power can be protective and
nurturing.)

> Praise Ishtar, the most glorious
> goddess,
> Let her be revered amongst men.
> Pleasure and love are her garments,
> She is clothed with life, grace and
> voluptuousness.
> Her lips are sweet, her mouth gives life.
> When she appears, our joy is complete.
> The counsel of Ishtar is most excel-
> lent,
> She holds the fate of all things in her
> hand.

Her greatness cannot be equaled,
And her word is respected by all
creation.
Joy is born of her glance,
Her gaze brings power and strength,
protection and nurture.
She hearkens to compassion and
entreaty,
And protects those who call upon her
name.

All praise to you Ishtar,
Most beautiful of beings,
Whose eyes shine brightly,
Whose voice is like music.
Strong, illustrious and radiant,
We bask in your light.

ROMEO AND JULIET

～

Although not exactly deities, Shakespeare's "star-cross'd lovers" have become famous the world over as the archetype of romance. No matter that it was a doomed romance: the strength and depth of love between these two has become a benchmark for love affairs throughout time.

"Give me my Romeo; and when he shall die,
Take him and cut him out in little stars,
And he will make the face of heaven so fine
That all the world will be in love with night
And pay no worship to the garish sun."
                              (Act III, scene ii, 21)

What man *wouldn't* want to inspire such sentiments?

   Try your hand at poetry – even if it's not exactly a classic, the fact that you took the time and trouble to write it yourself is a sign of your love. And remember that love-letters are a beautiful way to weave little love-spells into your daily life – even if they are sent by e-mail!

TOTEMS

Certain birds and animals have a reputation for possessing qualities and characteristics which may prove helpful in your romantic life – either because they provide something that you feel is lacking, or simply as a symbol of your hopes and desires.

Images of these creatures – talismans – can be worn as jewelry (rings, pendants or earrings, for example), as carved figurines in your home or office, as tattoos (but be absolutely certain you're happy with the totem before you do anything so permanent) or you can even dress and make-up to symbolize the creature itself – if you have the nerve to do so!

Modern fabrics can create the effect of iridescent feathers or scales, and there are plenty of realistic-looking fake furs available (we wouldn't endorse the use of real fur), while modern cosmetics provide plenty of vibrant color for face, body and hair. You are only limited by your imagination . . .

SWAN

~

The swan symbolizes the epitome of romantic love. Beautiful, graceful and lordly, the sight of swans on a tranquil stretch of river is enough to stir even the most jaded soul.

Swans are faithful birds, and make tender, caring parents. They are also fiercely protective of their mates and brood. Their reputation of mating for life has made them the ideal totem for the couple who wish to keep their partnership strong and sure.

Swans "dance" during their courtship, creating living "heart" shapes with their heads and necks as they mirror each other's movements. To bring a little swan-magic into your life, try taking dance classes (old time or ballroom, though, not line dancing or disco!)

DOVE

~

The dove is special to Aphrodite, and is representative of the sweetness of young love (young in the sense of new and fresh rather than just for young people). Their soft, cooing call is one of the delights of summer, and has led to the phrase "billing and cooing."

Keep a statuette of a pair of doves near the entrance to your home, to help safeguard your domestic happiness. But remember that dove-magic is gentle and homely, so don't keep images – or the birds themselves – if you want excitement in your life.

To help reconcile yourself to the loss of a lover, buy a dove and set it free.

PEACOCK

~

Included here more as a warning! The peacock is one of the most impressive and beautiful of all birds, but it also has the reputation of being vain, silly and pretentious. Its purpose is purely decorative, and it has a loud and ugly voice.

If you find yourself attracted to the human version of the peacock, as many people do, you may find you have to fight for their attention. However, if you wish to bring a little glamor into your own life, try owning a peacock feather fan or a luxurious, peacock-colored article of clothing. Do try not to imitate either the bird or its human counterpart, though, or you could end up looking foolish!

DEER

～

Deer are often seen as symbolic of the softer, gentler side of nature. An attractive epithet for a loving, tender woman is "doe-eyed" (the aggressive behavior of the stags in the rutting season tends to be largely ignored in such idealistic contemplation!) In Chinese lore, the deer symbolizes immortality, and may be viewed as representing an undying relationship.

In considering deer-magic, it is important to be very sure that the relationship is one you wish to continue, since once invoked, it is difficult to cancel — and you may find yourself trapped in an unhappy situation with no way out.

CATS AND DOGS

There are many different sorts of cats and dogs, and each has its own magic. The following pages give brief details of some of the better known.

It's worth remembering that in the main, cats are solitary beasts, and ideal totems for single people (and those who are determined to stay that way!), while dogs are pack animals — regardless of the legendary reputation of the "lone wolf"!

LION

~

The lion has the reputation of being the king of the beasts, but actually this epithet is somewhat misplaced. Lions may *look* regal, but it is the lioness that hunts and provides the food: the lion is something of a parasite, mostly dependent on the female for his existence. As a totem, the lioness is far more appropriate, especially for the single woman looking for an exciting, but not necessarily permanent, relationship. That being said, a full, mane-like hairstyle may prove very effective as a charm to generate lion-magic.

If possible wear jewelry resembling claws and teeth (but preferably not the real thing), and sleek tawny-colored clothing. Practice a direct, business-like approach to people, and accept admiration as your due!

TIGER

~

"Tyger! Tyger! Burning bright
In the forests of the night,
What immortal hand or eye
Could frame thy fearful symmetry?"
                         William Blake

If the lion is the king of the African plains,
the tiger is his equal in the Asian forests.
Noble, sensitive and courageous, the tiger is
the perfect totem for the person (male or
female) who – through choice or happen-
stance – lives a solitary life but still wants a
romantic attachment. Tiger's eye (the beautiful semi-precious stone) set in gold makes
perfect jewelry for such a person. Wearing
clothes with subtle stripes and shading may
also help to generate tiger-magic.

DOMESTIC CATS

∽

The household cat comes in a vast array of pattern, colors and temperaments! Simply owning one of these lovely felines adds cat-magic to your life: the breed says a great deal about the sort of person you are (or want to be!) A silver tabby, for example, is a little like a scaled-down tiger, suggesting hints of wildness beneath the surface, while a Siamese implies breeding, refinement and a touch of arrogance. Burmese — in fact most of the longhaired breeds — symbolize luxury and gracious living. Black cats are myste-rious, bewitching creatures, and very often the enchantment rubs off on their humans!

And of course, there is always the kitten — playful, impish, mischievous, the sort of small creature that people just can't help loving and wanting to look after . . . Some cats remain kittens all their lives, and are delightfully youthful well into old age.

Obviously, owning a cat (or having it own you, which is more often true) is a big responsibility and not to be undertaken lightly – and there is always the risk that your intended beloved doesn't like cats (in which case perhaps you should consider choosing a different lover!) But cats bring love into your life, and if you feel loved, and relaxed, you will automatically become more attractive to others – and that's where the true magic of the love spell lies!

WOLF

~

The wolf represents the strong protector: it symbolizes wildness, the natural world and inner strength. Traditionally, it is also seen as a helpful guide, especially for the lost traveler. Although usually viewed as a dangerous predator, in the sphere of love-magic the wolf can act as a totem of protection in a tense situation or relationship.

Due in part to the wolf's significance in Native American lore, in the absence of more obvious wolf imagery Amerindian silver and turquoise jewelry may be worn talismanically to help bring the animal's influence into your life.

FOX

~

The fox is a shrewd and clever animal, with a reputation for being able to extricate itself from tricky situations – the ideal symbol for those who are forever finding themselves tangled up in complicated love lives!

It's usually not too difficult to find representations of the fox, either as jewelry, on clothing, or even key-rings: you might find it useful to use one of these latter for your car keys (to help you make a quick escape from awkward situations . . .) In such circumstances, you might also find it helpful to address a quick petition to the spirit of the fox, perhaps asking that you not be found out!

DOG

~

The domestic dog comes in an enormous range of sizes, shapes and colors, even more so than the cat. As with the cat, the breed you choose can represent either the sort of person you are or how you would like to be seen, but whereas another person will only get to know your cat once they've been welcomed into your home, a dog is admired in the outside world, and is often a more obvious symbol of your personality. The stylish Afghan, for example, presents a completely different image than does a pugnacious Jack Russell, a sporty Retriever, or a snooty Pekinese: and you can use these visual clues not only to express your own personality, but also to give you an insight into the nature of potential lovers!

Dogs are far less independent animals

than cats, and require a lot more care and company. They are also blindly affectionate, and will repay many-fold love you give them, unconditionally and without asking for much more than food, walks and the occasional hug in return. If you truly find it difficult to find your ideal human love, but (like most of us) need a loving companion, a dog may prove to be, not, of course, a substitute, but nevertheless a cherished friend.

FLOWER MAGIC

~⚜~

Just about everyone knows that a red rose is a symbol of love — but did you know that most other flowers — and some fruits — also carry hidden meanings?

Although little used today, a complete "Language of Flowers" was devised during the last 150 years, allowing lovers to send secret messages to each other. In the following pages you'll learn how to tell your beloved how you feel about them, and how they feel about you! Learn this magical language, and let flower spells work for you . . .

FIRST ATTEMPTS . . .

∿

There are some delightful ways to flirt using flowers – though you need to be careful to use the right ones! And it's not necessary to spend a fortune at the florist: a lot of common garden plants or wildflowers have their own meanings too. (But you should always be wary of the color yellow when sending flowers . . .).

On first meeting someone who makes your heart miss a beat, try giving them a red carnation – it means "Ah! my poor heart – I am smitten!"

You could hope to receive a cheerful bunch of celandines in return – they symbolize "pleasures and happiness to come," while the simple garden daisy indicates that the giver shares your feelings.

But a striped carnation means, "I refuse

your advances," while a yellow indicates that the object of your affection holds you in disdain: depending on the strength of your feelings, it might be better to try elsewhere. And if you are given basil, you'd better give up altogether – it might be the king of herbs, but in the language of flowers it means, "I hate you"!

However, a single white rosebud is a hopeful sign: it means that the giver's heart is innocent and hasn't yet known love. Perhaps you are the person to teach them its joys . . .

TREES AND SHRUBS

~

There are quite a few trees and shrubs to choose from if you want to let your beloved know which of their qualities you admire.

A spray of elm leaves symbolizes dignity, while the rowan represents prudence.

A birch twig symbolizes meekness, and a spray from the black poplar says that you delight in their courageous spirit. A sprig of holly means you admire their foresight, while larch leaves let them know you think them bold and audacious!

Leaves from the beech tree symbolize riches, and can be seen as a lucky charm if exchanged between lovers. A twig from the box tree suggests that you will be stoical and staunch in your love, regardless of how the other responds, while a cedar twig symbolizes strength and enduring love.

A sprig from the elder tree tells your lover that you are zealous in your feelings – but be wary of giving sweet-scented linden flowers: they symbolize conjugal love and could be taken as a proposal of marriage!

Lilac, that lovely, fragrant, flowering shrub, sends several messages. White lilac expresses the innocence of youth; the mauve or light purple lilac symbolizes young love, while the deep purple variety may be exchanged between lovers in a long-term relationship to reaffirm their love.

There are also ways to let your beloved know you love them for their mind! Clematis sends the message, "your mind and imagination are beautiful," while a single dahlia indicates that you think they have excellent taste! Laburnum flowers tell your beloved they are a pensive beauty – but make sure they aren't wilted: dying laburnum flowers mean you feel yourself forsaken and hopeless in love.

HERBS AND VEGETABLES

~

While perhaps not the most apparent floral tributes, nevertheless some herbs and vegetables can express your feelings as well as a bunch of flowers – and in a less obvious fashion. So if you wish to be subtle, try some of these . . .

An ancient way to use the lovely blue flowers of borage is to float them in a glass of wine. Borage represents blunt speaking, and indicates that everything you are about to say should be taken seriously – so make sure you mean it! Rue symbolizes disdain, and rosemary remembrance: the latter may be given in memory of good times you have spent together. Sweet basil indicates "good wishes," while chervil symbolizes sincerity: in combination with sorrel ("fondness") or – even better – wood sorrel ("joy"), such a posy is a charming and heartfelt wish for good luck and happiness.

Coriander indicates that you have a secret to tell, or that there are hidden qualities under a flippant exterior. Cress represents a promise of stability, while angelica tells the other that they inspire you. Bay leaves promise that you will be faithful to the end, while fennel tells your beloved you think them worthy of everyone's praises. Sage symbolizes great esteem, while peppermint expresses the true warmth of your feelings.

Strawberry flowers express the expectation of good times ahead – raspberries symbolize remorse and may be given as an apology. Be wary of blackberries, though – they symbolize envy. Peaches are an ideal gift to receive – they mean that the giver thinks your beauty, charm and good qualities are unequalled. Cherries represent youthful vitality, while pears represent warm affection.

Sweet chestnut expresses a wish for your lover's life to be filled with luxuries, and walnuts indicate a respect for their intellect. Lemons mean, "you bring vitality to my life"; apples symbolize temptation; and the pineapple tells your beloved that you think they are perfect. Turnips represent a charitable nature, while truffles indicate a surprise in the offing; mushrooms, however, symbolize suspicion, so employ them with care. The potato symbolizes benevolence and magnanimity. Even the humble cabbage has a meaning – "we will profit from our partnership!"

ROSES

~

Roses symbolize love in all its forms, and the language of roses almost deserves a book to itself! However, the following short list should enable you to pick your way through the minefield . . .

A single rose – I love you – pure and simple.

Thornless rose – I have loved you since I first saw you.

White rose – I am worthy of you. (Alternatively – You are a heavenly creature.)

Pink rose – You are graceful and elegant.

Red rose – symbolizes happy love.

Deep red rose – symbolizes bashful love, secret love.

Purple-red rose – You don't know how lovely you are!

Cream rose – Your beauty is forever new . . .

"Blue" rose – Meet me by moonlight.

Orange rose – I am infatuated with you.

Coral-colored rose – symbolizes sexual desire.

Yellow rose – I grow tired of you. (Alternatively – I am jealous.)

Red and white roses together – We are united in love.

Striped roses – We are at war.

Wild rose – The joy of loving you is mixed with pain.

Musk rose – You are beautiful but capricious. (I wish you'd make up your mind!)

"Cabbage" rose (old-fashioned variety – large with lots of petals) – Please be my love.

Opened rose in a bunch with two rosebuds – Keep our love a secret.

Single red rosebud – You are truly beautiful, the prize of my heart.

Single white rosebud – symbolizes a pure heart, one that has not yet known love.

Bouquet of rosebuds – symbolizes innocent love.

Bouquet of opened white roses and rosebuds – You are too pure and angelic for earthly love. (Not recommended for hopeful lovers!)

FOR A MORE LIMITED BUDGET AND SIMPLER TASTES…

~

Chrysanthemums represent cheerfulness, especially in difficult times: choose red for sturdy love, or white for honesty (yellow indicates you feel yourself slighted and is probably best avoided). Lily of the valley symbolizes a return to happiness and is a charming gift to receive from a lover after you've been away. Pansies represent thoughts – blue for "I miss you," purple means "you fill my life with riches," orange symbolizes warm hugs, while the multi-colored, "face" varieties express hope that the recipient is feeling happy. Wild pansies – heartsease – symbolize "you are always in my thoughts."

White clover says, "think of me," while red clover means, "don't work too hard!": a four-leafed clover means, "please be my love."

Honeysuckle expresses admiration for the recipient's sweet disposition and a hope that love will always be true. Ivy symbolizes friendship and faithfulness; a sprig of ivy with its tendrils indicates that you are eager to please them. Lunaria (Honesty) represents truth and sincerity, as does fern; and daffodils express deep regard for the beloved.

Iris says you have a message to give your lover, but would prefer to do so in person. Enchanter's nightshade, that charming little wildflower of the woods, tells your beloved that they fascinate and bewitch you. Bluebells symbolize constant affection, and are reputed to make the bearer speak only the truth . . .

A simple dock leaf symbolizes that you will wait patiently for your love, while mistletoe, especially out of season, tells them you will overcome all difficulties to win their heart. (In season – at Yuletide – it becomes a fertility symbol, and kissing below it brings good luck.)

If your lover sends you yellow tulips ("your love has no chance of success"), try responding with stinging nettles; they symbolize, "you are too cruel." Hopefully you will receive hazelnuts – "let us be reconciled" – in return!

The Legend of the Forget-me-not

~

Forget-me-not, the lover's flower, means "I love you truly – do not forget me." The legend behind this bright blue flower's name is a delightful, if sad, tale:

A knight in armor and his lady were walking by a river when the lady spied some pretty blue flowers growing by the water. She admired them, and the knight went to pick them for her. Alas, his armor unbalanced him, and he tumbled into the water, still clutching the flowers. As he went under for the third and last time, he threw the flowers to his love, crying "Forget-me-not . . ."

(The legend doesn't say what happened to the lady. We may hope that she stayed true to his wish!)

Of course, if you want to get a less favorable message across, there are other plants to choose.

Maple leaves indicate that the giver is unsure of the situation and would prefer to wait and see, while privet symbolizes prohibitions and denial: though useful as a hedging plant, it's not recommended for bouquets! Dead leaves symbolize melancholic sadness: the dead leaves of specific trees or shrubs indicate the death of the quality or feeling that plant represents.

Crab-apple blossom lets the recipient know you think them ill natured, while giving hops, or the gentian flower, means that you feel you have been treated unjustly. Purple hyacinth symbolizes sorrow: it can be given either to say "sorry," or to express distress at the other's behavior. If you want to be tacitly rude, you can always have a small bunch of redcurrants delivered: their message ("you please everyone") is two-edged, meaning either "everyone likes you," or something a lot less flattering!

While lavender is renowned for its healing abilities and lovely old-world fragrance, it's not overly welcome as a floral tribute — in the language of flowers it means "I don't fully trust you." Mind you, that could be useful as a warning to mend your ways! Convolvulous symbolizes uncertainty and a fear of being trapped in a relationship. And to extricate yourself from a relationship where the other is clinging, try sending sweetbrier: it means, "I wound in order to heal — I am no longer yours."

FINALLY, PLANTS TO AVOID –
UNLESS YOU REALLY
MEAN IT!

≈

Foxglove – symbolizes insincerity.

Laurel flowers – "Perfidious one! Get far from me . . ."

Lettuce – "You are unfeeling and frigid" (obviously, this doesn't apply if all you did was go shopping for salad makings . . .).

Willow herb – "You are unbelievably pretentious!"

Weeping willow – symbolizes mourning, and especially bereavement. Best avoided . . .

Tansy – symbolizes a declaration of intense hostility against the other.

A single almond – symbolizes stupidity and indiscretion.

Lobelia – a symbol of unadulterated malevolence . . .

DIVINATION

~❦~

Most of us would like to know what the future
has in store for us, both so that we know what to
expect and so that we can prepare for misfortune
– hence the vast number of forms of divination
available to anyone who cares to search. In the
following pages are some of the ways that lovers
through the ages have tried to divine the course
of their loves. Some are quick and easy, some
require a little more effort, but all can be tried by
anyone wishing for a glimpse into the future. But
be warned – there is no guarantee that any of
them can accurately foretell what is to come!

FIRE

~

Touch a corner of a love-letter to a flame (or use the envelope if the letter is too precious to burn). If the flame is strong and bright, the relationship, and your lover, is staunch and true. However, if it is meager, or goes out, or won't light at all, then beware — regardless of the words, the relationship is all but dead.

A variation of this is to write the name of your lover on a piece of paper and hold it to the flame of a white candle. Again, a reluctant flame indicates a dying relationship, and a strong flame a strong love — but if the paper flares and burns to ash almost immediately, beware: too hot a passion dies quickly!

Take a red (if you're female) or green (if you're male) candle and push a pin into it, about half way down. Light the candle and time how long it takes to burn down far enough for the pin to fall. The longer the time, the stronger the love, and the longer it will last. If the pin doesn't fall from the candle, but slowly slides down the side, you are likely to remain together for the rest of your lives . . .

AIR

~

Sneezes have been used in a counting rhyme to foretell the romantic prospects for the next few days . . .

"One sneeze – a kiss
Two – a wish come true
Three – a love letter
Four – something even better!"

Presumably sneezing more than four times means you have a cold, and are out of the romantic running until it's cleared up!

There is an older variant of the rhyme:

"Sneeze on a Monday, sneeze for danger;
Sneeze on a Tuesday, kiss a stranger;
Sneeze on a Wednesday, expect a letter;
Sneeze on a Thursday for something better;
Sneeze on a Friday, sneeze for sorrow;
Sneeze on a Saturday, see your sweetheart tomorrow;
Sneeze on a Sunday, your safety seek –
Bad luck will dog you the whole of the week."

If you are single and looking for a partner, try bird watching on St Valentine's day. A superstition states that the bird you see first on February 14 foretells the status and occupation of your future mate:

Blackbird – an older man or woman, in business or religion.

Magpie or Jay – a charming rogue who'll steal your heart away – and leave you lonely.

Robin – a cheerful person, in one of the caring professions.

Pigeon or Dove – a good, honest, loving person, one who works with their hands or for the good of the planet.

Hen or Duck – a homemaker, brusque, efficient and kindly.

Tit or Finch – a younger person, possibly flighty, difficult to pin down but a lot of fun!

Owl – an older person, in the legal or academic professions.

Sparrow or Starling – a homely person of little ambition but much endurance.

Swan – a dignified person, one who travels a lot.

Hawk or Eagle – a noble, high-principled person, possibly connected with the armed forces.

Crow or Rook – a strict, careful man or woman, in banking, insurance or other financial business.

Exotic bird (macaw, cockatoo etc.) – an extravagant person, an actor or artist.

WATER

~

Next time you have a cup of tea or coffee, look carefully at the surface. If there are bubbles floating, there is a kiss coming your way in the very near future! Inviting someone to join you in a cappuccino could, therefore, be either the prelude to a romantic interlude, or a dangerous occupation . . .

Putting milk or cream in the tea or coffee before you add the sugar or honey is an omen of lost love – although, of course, if you don't take a sweetener you can ignore this one. Furthermore, if two spoons are accidentally placed on one saucer, it's a sign of a wedding in the near future!

EARTH

~

To find out if your future mate will be dark or fair-haired, take a table knife with a white handle and spin it in a circle on a table. If it stops with the blade towards you, your lover will be dark-haired: if with the haft, expect a blond! (If it falls off the table it warns of the abrupt end to the romance.)

It's a very good omen if your hand shakes while you write a love letter – and if you should blot the letter (not a common occurrence unless you write with a pen using real ink) even better: it presages happiness in the very near future.

For an unusual divination, scratch the names of possible lovers on pieces of cheese and leave them somewhere cool. The first piece that becomes moldy is the ideal lover!

Alternatively, you can leave the cheese pieces in the cage of a mouse or rat. The first piece that is eaten then represents the person on whom you should concentrate your affections.

PLANTS

~

If you are in the enviable position of having numerous people from which to choose your partner, but unable to make up your mind, you could try taking one onion for each of your potential lovers. Scratch the name of each one on an onion, then leave the bulbs somewhere warm. The first one to sprout will reveal the name of the person it would be best for you to marry.

A rather more grisly method of divination, for women, involves going to a churchyard at midnight and throwing a handful of small seeds – mustard or poppy – over your left shoulder. You may then see behind you the ghostly image of your future lover, mowing with an old-fashioned scythe . . .

Another way to see an apparition of your future intended is to take a willow stick in your left hand, leave the house without anyone else seeing you, and run three times around the house saying – "The one who's to be my [man/woman] come and grip the other end." On the third turn, the ghost of the partner may be seen holding the other end of the stick.

To forecast whether a partnership will be successful or not, the couple should each drop an acorn into a bowl of water. If the acorns float towards each other, love and luck are assured. If they float apart, however, stormy times and arguments are ahead.

The ash tree has quite a reputation for promoting love: the leaves represent loyalty, friendship and warm companionship, while the seeds are considered to be an aphrodisiac (when carried or exchanged, NOT eaten!)

Pick a handful of the leaves, saying as you do so:

> "Lovely ash, these leaves I pluck,
> Grant that they may bring me luck:
> That, tonight, in dreams I see
> The one who is my love to be."

Sleep with them under your pillow!

MOON OMENS FOR WOMEN

~

A woman who has been unlucky in love over the past year could try going secretly out into a garden on the first new moon of the year, and brush her hair, mentally reciting:

> "New moon, I salute you, please show to me
> The face of the man who's my lover to be."

As long as she remains silent until she is in bed, she should dream of her future lover that night.

To find out how long it will be before you find true love, stand on a stone with your back to the full moon and look into a mirror. The number of reflected moons you see represent the number of months until you meet your lover.

KISSES

~

A kiss on the nose is unlucky and means there is an argument just waiting to happen between the pair.

If, when kissing a man with a mustache, a hair is left on the lips, it presages a lonely future. (You could always comb the mustache first, to remove any loose hair and the curse!)

To refuse to kiss under the mistletoe will cause bad luck in love.

There is a curious belief in some parts of the world that every kiss you give takes a minute off your life. Presumably this would mean that every kiss you receive adds a minute – so aim for equality of numbers!

YOUR FORTUNE IN
YOUR HAND

~•~

Palmistry is an ancient and respected method of divination, using the lines and marks on the hands to give an insight into individual character and destiny. It's a big subject, beyond the scope of this little book, so in the following pages we'll only touch on those particular features that relate directly to romance and love, and only in the simplest terms.

   Note that traditionally, the left hand represents traits you were born with, while the right hand reveals those characteristics that you have acquired throughout your life. If you are naturally left-handed, the reverse applies.

YOUR HAND

~

As far as your love life is concerned, there are three main features in the palm – yours or your partners – to investigate. These are:

1. The Line of the Heart
2. The Mount of Venus
3. The Lines of Affection (or Marriage, or Partnership)

(You should also note the Line of the Head – 4.)

To see where these are situated on your hand, please see the illustration on the opposite page.

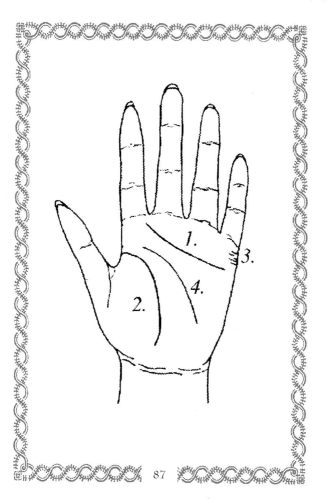

The Heart Line

~

If this starts below the index finger, it denotes an individual who loves deeply, is reliable and faithful, but has a tendency to idealize their beloved! Such a person tends to place lovers on a pedestal, and is often disappointed and hurt when they prove themselves human and fallible.

A Heart Line starting in between the index and middle fingers indicates a calm, open-eyed attitude to romance: while capable of profound affection, such a person has no illusions about love.

In the Heart Line which starts below the middle finger, there is a risk of the individual being possessive of lovers and prone to jealousy.

Generally speaking, clearly defined lines indicate a healthy attitude and straightforward, uncomplicated responses. A smooth, deep, cleanly etched Heart Line indicates a smooth love life and consistent affections. A thin, lightly etched Heart Line denotes coolness, selfishness and lack of emotional depth. A broad but shallow Heart Line indicates a fickle, superficial individual where romance is concerned – one who may have several lovers at the same time.

A fork at the end of the line strengthens its overall effect. A chain-like formation along the length of the line indicates changeable affections and a dislike of staying true to one person: on the hand of a person with a strong, deep Heart Line, this can lead to emotional conflicts and a lot of unhappiness. Small breaks and gaps in the line indicate romantic failures and disappointments.

Finally, if the Heart Line is low down on the hand, close to the Head Line, the emotions are likely to interfere with the intellect (the heart will rule the head). If it's high on the hand, close to the fingers, and the Head Line lies close to it, the opposite will apply, indicating a cold, manipulative individual who uses the love of others to further their own ends.

The Mount of Venus

~

Generally speaking, a large, high, well-rounded Mount of Venus denotes someone who is happy with their sexuality and possesses considerable personal magnetism (whether they could actually be called attractive or not is immaterial!). Such a person is generous, hospitable, and often very popular.

If a large Mount of Venus is found on a soft and flabby hand, however, it indicates a lazy individual, one who is happy to let the partner do all the work in the relationship, and whose passion is often quickly exhausted.

On the other hand, a flat, narrow Mount of Venus usually indicates sexual insecurity and diffidence with the other sex. They may have a tendency to overcompensate by becoming dismissive of or hostile to others (depending on other factors – their physical appearance, talents, etc. – this may sometimes be taken as a challenge, and such a person might find themselves on the receiving end of some determined efforts to break down their reserve!).

A smooth, firm Mount of Venus is associated with a person of refinement and taste, with a love of the arts, a moderate libido, and considerable self-control.

The Lines of Affection

~

These little lines, under the pinkie at the very edge of the hand, may be slight enough as to be almost invisible. For the casual palmist, they are less important than the Heart Line or Mount of Venus, but they can still provide an insight into the character.

Generally speaking, these lines indicate the number and strength of intimate relationships the person will experience through life. Lots of tiny, shallow lines denote a lot of pleasant but short-term romances: at the other extreme, one deep, strong line denotes a single life-long devotion to one person (or thing). Most people fall in between these two, with a number of little lines and one or two deeper ones, indicating several romances and a couple of more important partnerships. The closer the line(s) start to the Heart Line, the earlier the individual

will become aware of love and romance!
Lines that are broken or look like they are
full of little islands, warn of difficulties and
obstacles in your love life (if there is also a
strong, clear Heart Line, however, such
problems will be temporary).

As a last comment, traditionally, upright
lines on the Lines of Affection denote children – broad and strong denote boys, while
delicate and fine indicate girls. Since having
(or not having) children is far more a matter
of choice than in the past, such lines have
become less important these days . . .

DREAM LOVER

~❀~

Modern psychologists have joined ancient mystics in realizing the importance of our dreams. In view of the strength of the biological imperative of reproduction, it is not surprising that love and sex figure strongly in the dreams that reveal our subconscious mind, as well as in our waking thoughts.

The language of the subconscious is emotional rather than literal, and messages are couched in pictures rather than in words. In the dream world, the hat someone is wearing can be more important than the words they are saying!

Dreams and the images that clothe their secret truths may seem chaotic and random, but patient study can begin to unravel their *mysteries, and it is well worth while keeping a dream diary – if nothing else, it will make fascinating reading on a rainy day!*

Over the millennia, many researchers have sought to provide a dictionary of the language of dreams, and the following extracts from this continually evolving work have been chosen as being particularly relevant to deciphering subconscious hints and warnings about your love life.

It is important to realize however, that these dream definitions are suggested meanings only. The full interpretation of any dream is dependent both upon the atmosphere of the whole of the dream, and on the precise context in which the particular element appears.

Please note that the significance in dreams of many flowers and crystals can be derived from the meanings and uses of these items in the other sections of this book.

DREAMS

~

Abandonment – to abandon someone you dislike, at the altar for example, is a sign of forthcoming prosperity. If you liked him or her, though, you will need inner strength to win through difficulties. If you were abandoned, then look out for an opportunity too good to miss.

Accident at sea – this indicates difficulties in your love life.

Admiration – if you were being admired then take care not to become complacent and vain!

Aisle of a church – think carefully before you commit yourself!

Allspice – romance.

Apple – if the fruit is sweet then romance is in the air, if sour then disappointment lurks nearby.

Archery – if you are unattached then prepare for attachment! Otherwise you may need strength to resist an alluring stranger.

Bark of a tree – be cautious in dealings with the opposite sex.

Basin or bowl – if full with anything but clean water then expect disappointment from your lover.

Bereavement – if of a complete stranger then expect news of an engagement or even a wedding – perhaps your own!

Butterfly – romantic success and family happiness.

Capsule – success in relationships, the more the merrier.

Car – parking signifies the end of a relationship.

Cards – King of Hearts is true love; Queen of Hearts is romance; Jack of Hearts is an infatuation.

Champagne – at a wedding, this signifies romance and joy.

Cloven hoof – traditionally a sign of an embarrassing deception.

Cockatoo – don't listen to gossip, but if you do then don't repeat it maliciously!

Collar – if dirty or disheveled then trust is misplaced, if clean and tidy then your heart is in safe hands.

Comb – losing a comb indicates the loss to a rival of a loved one.

Comet – a chance encounter that leads to love.

Cone – a powerful symbol that signifies sensual and sexual pleasure.

Corkscrew – beware of emotional entanglements.

Crow – separation.

Cuckoo – misplaced trust.

Dancing couples – success in affairs of the heart.

Dice – if you are uncertain about a relationship, this dream image warns against simply trusting to luck for a happy ending.

Disgrace – curiously, the greater the disgrace the greater the success in love that is signified.

Donkey – sensual, sexual and even promiscuous liaisons are signified.

Dove – reciprocated love.

Drink – sweet drinks signify a passionate affair.

Duck and drake – romance.

Duet – romance and domestic bliss.

Ecstasy – an unsatisfying love life.

Elk – sexual activity.

Fingernails – long fingernails indicate that a relationship needs careful handling.

Fire – lighting a fire in a fireplace (or poking one) signifies sexual activity. Putting out a fire indicates that the fizz has gone out of a relationship.

Fireplace – if cold then dissatisfaction with a relationship is signified.

Flood – being swept away is a warning against misplacing your trust.

Florist – if you are unattached it indicates a new romance.

Freckles – you have admirers.

Gondola – a wish for romance.

Hammock – falling out is a warning not to take your partner for granted.

Hangover – beware of indiscretions.

Harem – sensual and sexual encounters are signified.

Hat – wearing a new hat indicates a new relationship; a hat that is too large warns of embarrassment; one that is too small signifies dissatisfaction.

Hedge – if verdant and lush then a successful love affair is signified.

Hothouse – a hothouse or conservatory, so long as it is in good condition, signifies an escalation of passion in a love affair.

Ice-skating – if with a partner, then beware of indiscretions.

Iguana – this is said to signify meeting unusual new friends...

Impotence – traditionally, this indicates an upsurge in activity in your love life.

Jungle – walking through one warns that an emotional entanglement is developing into a knotty problem!

Ketchup – a savory new friend.

Kitten – a frivolous affair.

Knot – untying a knot indicates the loosening of emotional bonds.

Lace – you have admirers of the opposite sex.

Lane – walking along a narrow lane is a warning to be discreet.

Lantern – a swinging light warns against imprudence.

Lock – fitting a key into one signifies satisfaction with your love life.

Lute – to see or hear this instrument signifies light-hearted romance.

Magician – the resurrection of a long-past love affair.

Magnet – sexual magnetism and prowess.

Marble – this stone signifies turbulence in a love affair.

Mermaid – this is a personification of your love life and, therefore, whatever was happening around the mermaid is indicative of what is happening to your love life.

Metal – lead signifies disappointment in love. Any alloy either signifies a happy marriage or, if you are married already, a new child.

Moon – the full moon signifies success in all matters of love. If the moon is reflected in the water of a lake then the success will be particularly romantic and profound.

Music – Deep and melodious organ music signifies sensuality and sexual satisfaction.

Musical instrument – carrying one which you do not play in waking life, signifies a fulfilling relationship.

Naked – in a public place, this signifies a break from routine and the chance to initiate a new relationship.

Name – if you can't remember your own name then take care that an illicit affair doesn't rob you of your reputation, your "good name."

Navel – the birth of a new affair of the heart.

Necklace – if beautiful, then the omens for a love affair are good.

Nightingale – either seen or heard, this bird is a herald of romance and domestic bliss.

Office – if it is the office where you work in your waking life, then it signifies that your love life is changing direction.

Omelet – if light and fluffy then an insubstantial but rapturous affair is signified.

Oyster – eating this shellfish signifies that a love affair is ripe for fulfillment.

Parachute – your trust is well placed (unless it failed to function properly, in which case your trust is *definitely* placed in the wrong hands).

Park – enjoying a public park signifies a happy love life.

Parrot – this warns that you may be hurt by gossip about you.

Perfume – Musk signifies a passionate love affair. A light, delicate scent signifies a delightful romantic interlude.

Pickle – satisfaction.

Poetry – you are interesting to the opposite sex.

Ring – finding or being given a ring signifies a new relationship.

Sandals – a new romance.

Scarf – a new scarf indicates a new romance.

Scissors – the end of a relationship.

Shawl – worn over your head, this signifies satisfaction within a relationship.

Skein – tangled threads signify romantic disappointment, but if it is tidy then fulfillment in love is signified.

Sled – a roller coaster ride of an affair!

Snake – traditionally, serpents warn against false friends. Specifically, they warn you against taking lovers for granted.

Spire – true love.

Spring – when dreamed of out of season, this signifies a renewal of romantic activity.

Springs – these coiled wires etc. signify inconstancy.

Stag – sexual activity.

Stairs – falling up them signifies good luck in love.

Swan – domestic bliss and romantic happiness.

Tickling – beware of frivolity that leads to indiscretion.

Torch – a firebrand is a sign of an incandescent love affair.

Tree – planting a tree is a sign of being ready for a new relationship.

Unicorn – the blossoming of romance into commitment.

Vacuum cleaner – successful dealings with the opposite sex.

Valentine card – receiving one signifies turbulence in affairs of the heart, whereas giving one indicates you are ready for new relationships.

SIMPLE SYNASTRY

Synastry is the astrological art of matching two individual horoscopes to measure the compatability (or otherwise!) of the people involved. Obviously, to gain a true picture it is necessary to cast the natal charts – but the following pages can give you some idea, in very general terms, how love and romance affect each of the Zodiac Signs. By checking your own Sign and that of your partner, you should be able to gain some idea of what to expect – and how to react!

ARIES IN LOVE

~

Man Forceful, passionate, uncompromising, easily bored! The male Aries has a tendency to place his beloved on a pedestal. To keep him interested, keep him surprised with changes of images, new ideas and novel things to do. If you want to keep him, never let yourself become predictable – and never let him think he owns you.

Woman Dominant, passionate, not always the most faithful of people! The female Aries loves a challenge, but may also see her partner as a contestant in a battle of wills. Play hard to get, treat her to unusual experiences and presents, and make sure you never become boring.

Suggested Gifts A day out at a safari or theme park; a disposable camera.

Charm to Attract an Aries

~

The best day to perform this spell is Thursday, and the best place a hilltop. Dress entirely in red, and wear red jewelry – especially rubies if you own any: the ruby is Aries' birth stone.

Take something made of iron – an iron nail, or, even better, a small piece of meteoric iron – and a single, bright red candle. If possible, light some citrus-scented incense (a joss stick is ideal if you're out of doors). Hold the lit candle and iron in front of you, and focus on the candle flame as you repeat, mentally: "[name], by fire and iron I conjure you to me."

Carry the iron with you at all times!

TAURUS IN LOVE

~

Man Stubborn, conservative, "physical," very down-to-earth and deeply concerned with quality. The male Taurus can also be extremely possessive: he likes to "own" his lovers. Behave like a lady, be faithful, and never interrupt him!

Woman Practical, luxury loving, calm, sensuous. The Taurean female is the archetypal "earth mother" and tower of strength. Defer to her common sense, don't play the field, and make sure any gifts are of good quality.

Suggested Gifts Discreet, classy jewelry; Belgian chocolates; a potted Bay Tree.

Charm to Win your Taurean

~

The best day to perform the spell is Friday: the best places a wildflower meadow or a rose garden. Wear deep green, and emeralds (or malachite) and a copper bangle to represent Venus, the ruler of the Sign.

The rose is the best talisman, preferably as jewelry (as a necklace, for example, or stylized cufflinks) but a scarf, tie or cravat are also appropriate. Hold the object gently to your throat, close your eyes and imagine the other standing with you, gazing into your eyes. If you can also imagine them saying "I love you," so much the better!

Wear the object next time you meet, but don't expect immediate results – Taurus takes these things slowly and carefully!

GEMINI IN LOVE
~

Man Funny, eloquent, fickle, often lacking in staying power! The male Gemini loves to talk, about anything and everything – don't be upset if he insists on answering the phone in the middle of a canoodling session! Romance should be playful, and may be more successful if you take charge . . .

Woman Chatty, flirtatious, teasing, great fun to be with. The Gemini female is generally fashionable, well informed, and restless. Keep your conversation light and stimulating: don't try to curb her vivacity (or caprice), and allow her her freedom if you want her to stay.

Suggested Gifts Internet access or a domain of their own; a mobile phone; a palmtop computer.

Charm to Entice a Gemini

~

An ongoing spell, this, and one that requires work. The best way to woo and win a Gemini is to show yourself to be a fascinating person. Find out the Gemini's address or phone number – or, more likely, their e-mail address – and every few days send them an interesting or unusual snippet of information, or a joke (nothing smutty, please), or an amusing anecdote or poem. Gemini loves puns, and information for its own sake, and often has an eccentric sense of humor; if you can match their sparkling wit you'll have a head start in the romantic stakes. But remember, to keep them, you'll need to continue in the same vein . . .

CANCER IN LOVE

~

Man Home loving, quiet, fiercely protective, deeply affectionate. The Cancer male is usually very tender, and relishes intimacy. Cherish him, buy him intimate little gifts, and bear with his occasional moods – but don't mother him, or you risk his acting like a temperamental adolescent!

Woman Maternal, moody, nostalgic, enigmatic. The Cancer female is a very "womanly" woman, sensitive and easily hurt. Be gentle, sympathetic, and a shoulder to cry on. And don't be surprised if she defends you like a tiger against anyone who slights you!

Suggested Gifts An antique mirror, silver photo-frame, hip flask or rag doll; lockable diary.

Charm to Woo your Cancer Lover

~

Monday is the best day, and the seashore the best place (try an aquarium if the sea is too far away): any time between new and full moon is appropriate. Wear white clothing and silver and moonstone jewelry. Take with you two small matching pieces of wearable silver (preferably rings, but a neckchain or bracelet are also appropriate).

Hold both pieces touching, in your cupped hands, and repeat, mentally:

"[name] as the moon draws the sea, may this silver draw you to me: may the power of the sweeping tide keep you always by my side."

Wear one piece and give the other to your prospective lover as a gift.

LEO IN LOVE

~

Man Magnanimous, wholehearted, generous, a little overwhelming. The Leo man usually expects to be the center of his own "court" of friends – a position he will share with his lover. Be properly appreciative, but don't be surprised if he outshines you!

Woman Loyal, sophisticated, dignified, often wants to share her happiness with the entire world – which is fine unless you want to keep it a secret! The Leo female expects fidelity and respect. Treat her like a queen, and she'll be gracious and loving in return.

Suggested Gifts Anything gold or gold-colored.

Charm to Capture your Lion

~

Sunday is the best day: the best place is a theater, art gallery or zoo. Wear gold or yellow colored clothing, and gold and diamond (or tiger's eye) jewelry – and take a packet of sunflower seeds with you . . .

Write the name of your hoped-for lover on the seed packet, and hold it tightly while enjoying the play/admiring the artworks/ watching the big cats. Later, plant the seeds in a sunny spot and visit them regularly, willing your intended's love to grow as the seedlings shoot towards the sun.

Save the seeds of the tallest sunflower to plant next year, to keep your relationship blooming!

VIRGO IN LOVE

~

Man Discriminating, interested in how you feel, and why; may insist on using manuals rather than trusting his own feelings! The Virgo male is usually self-controlled, and hates emotional scenes. Be natural and loving, encourage him to relax, and try to go for walks as often as possible.

Woman Cool, cautious, intelligent, may be a little suspicious of your motives. The Virgo female is competent and capable, and demands a considerable amount of personal space. Be her friend, respect her talents, and share your ideas over mugs of herbal tea!

Suggested Gifts A personal organizer; an aromatherapy or shiatsu course.

Charm to Engage a Virgo

~

Wednesday is the best day, and a library the ideal place, to perform the first part of this spell. Wear very pale yellow clothing and take a small lidded tin and a piece of rock crystal with you. Hold the crystal tightly, imagining the face of your chosen Virgo: if possible, imagine holding a conversation with them, telling them quietly and calmly how you feel.

When you feel you have explained your feelings sufficiently, wrap the crystal in a small piece of cotton and place it in the tin. As soon as you can, bury the closed tin in a private spot – a favorite place in the country or a secluded corner of a garden.

LIBRA IN LOVE

~

Man Gentle, eager to please, sometimes shy. The Libra male can be a perfectionist: his idea of romance is often a courtly, platonic affair. Engage him in discussion and debate rather than chat, and take an interest in his hobbies.

Woman Quiet, competent, intellectually inclined yet deeply romantic. The Libra female's intellect can be a little frightening to those who simply want a good time. Talk to her, accept the contradictory elements of her nature, and let her know how special she is.

Suggested Gifts A weekend away at a good hotel with excellent food; a sensual massage.

Charm to Charm a Libra Lover

~

Before performing the charm you'll need to find something that represents a bridge, or something with the Libra sigil on it. Friday is the best day; the best place is a well-kept garden or an old apple orchard. Wear shades of pale green, and carry a chrysoprase if possible.

Focus on your chosen object while thinking of the other person. Imagine a bridge being built between yourself and the other person, with a two-way flow of communication and ideas passing over it. Memorize this image, and call it to mind every time you are with the Libra.

SCORPIO IN LOVE

~

Man Dramatic, wickedly exciting, electrifying. The Scorpio male is possessive, but respects strength in others. He's also extremely attractive to others, so swallow your jealousy! Be adventurous, be loyal, and expect a thrilling (occasionally stormy) time . . .

Woman Fascinating, sensual, stimulating. The female Scorpio is secretive, needs to be in control, and has enormous will power. Be honest, emotionally open, and whatever you do, don't be possessive. Show her you're proud of her, but do be aware that the relationship may well be a little tempestuous.

Suggested Gifts Silk or velvet clothing (tasteful items, please!); a luxury cruise.

Charm to Intrigue your Scorpio

~

There is no particular "best day" to perform this charm, but the best time would be midnight. Wear black and dark red. Take a small representation of an eagle (a piece of jewelry, a little figurine, or – if you're lucky enough to have one – an eagle feather) to a lonely, deserted place; an actual desert is ideal (but please do make sure that you will be safe, wherever you decide).

Holding the symbol, envisage yourself becoming filled with controlled power, strength, and sheer determination – you'll need it if you plan a long-term relationship with a Scorpio! Carry it with you at all times to remind you of the qualities you need.

SAGITTARIUS IN LOVE

~

Man Outgoing, bold, adventurous, extravagant. The male Sagittarius needs to feel free – or at least not caged within a restrictive relationship. Be relaxed and optimistic with him, and you may find yourself on the journey of a lifetime.

Woman Restless, blunt, humorous, a good communicator. The Sagittarius female has a great love of the unknown and a sense of the magical qualities of life. Try to tie her down and she'll run a mile: share her adventures and you stand a good chance of a truly exciting and enlivening life.

Suggested Gifts Multi-blade penknife; waterproof, shockproof, multi-function watch.

Charm to Lure your Sagittarius

~

Thursday is the best day, and an airport or train station – or an ancient wood – the best place. Wear royal blue (something sporty or connected with travel is ideal) and slip a tumble-polished sodalite into your pocket. Take two small compasses with you: hold them side by side while saying mentally:

"[name], let me be your pole star. As this compass helps you on your quest through life, may it always bring you back to me."

If you want to be extravagant, buy compasses with metal covers, and have them engraved with your names. Keep your own and give the other to your Sagittarian – tell them it's for luck and they should always carry it with them!

CAPRICORN IN LOVE

～

Man Single-minded, manipulative, pragmatic, ruthless. The Capricorn male often finds it difficult to express emotion, and needs to be the strong half of the partnership. Share his interests, but don't expect to be the most important thing in his life – and don't be too surprised if he leaves in pursuit of someone with more youth, wealth or social status (especially if you're strongly independent yourself)!

Woman Cautious, self-controlled, serious, reserved. In serious relationships, the Capricorn female tends to look for a good father rather than a lover. Treat her with respect, prove that you are a good provider, and don't expect her to share her secrets.

Suggested Gifts Shares in a large company; a lockable diary.

Charm to Entice a Capricorn

~

Saturday is the best day for this charm: the best places are mountains (especially near lakes), or a bank or the offices of a successful large company. Wear black.

You will need to take some money with you, a minimum of three coins – small denominations or old money are quite sufficient (if you wish to wear the charm afterwards, have holes drilled so you can mount the coins on discreet earrings, a neckchain or bracelet). Name the coins – one for you, one for your intended, and one for Fate: symbolically set Fate free (drop it near the building, bury it in the soil, or throw it into the water). Keep the other two coins safe.

AQUARIUS IN LOVE

~

Man Innovative, unusual, disconcerting. Friendship — and personal freedom — is usually more important than love to Aquarius. Maintain a strong sense of your own identity and worth, expect endless and fascinating discussions, and don't make emotional scenes.

Woman Inspiring, startling, unique, highly independent. The Aquarius female deals with all comers with integrity, and can be brutally honest. Don't expect blind devotion, or fidelity, and it might be best to be prepared for an unusual relationship . . .

Suggested Gifts A night out to see a top illusionist, followed by an all-night party; a kinetic sculpture or plasma globe.

Charm to Beguile an Aquarius

~

Your best course of action is to work on yourself. Sharpen your mind, read up on current affairs, find out which causes your intended lover supports and research them (and choose a few of your own!), develop a rational, cool approach to discussion. It's also important to build a strong wall around your own emotions — learn not to let the unflattering truth upset you, and curb your possessiveness or jealousy. Aquarians deal fairly with all people, but have great difficulty in expressing their deeper feelings, and will show their love by defending your point of view, or by taking care of you, rather than with flowers, anniversary cards or expressions of devotion.

PISCES IN LOVE

~

Man Unwilling to take responsibility, dreamy, vacillating. The male Pisces responds to harsh or continual demands by disappearing. He'll share your deepest secrets, dreams and fears – but don't try to tie him down . . .

Woman Unpredictable, imaginative, secretive. The Pisces female can never be "owned" – but she may allow you to share a little of the profound depths in which she lives. Never take her for granted. And never lie to her.

Suggested Gifts Something very personal – a handwritten love poem or hand-drawn picture; a walk along a deserted seashore (preferably in the Maldives!)

Charm to Enchant a Pisces

～

Thursday is the best day: a cliff overlooking the sea – or on a boat – is the best place. Wear turquoise clothing – and take an exotic seashell with you.

Sit and meditate on the shell, its shape, its color and texture: think about the animal it once housed, and its place of origin. Imagine what it would feel like to be an aquatic creature, flowing with the tides, exploring the mysterious depths of the oceans, free to travel the world without limitations: this gives you an insight into the Piscean psyche. Focus that extraordinary feeling of freedom and mystery into the shell, and keep it by your bed to help you connect with your beloved.

YOUR FUTURE IN
YOUR CUP!

~ ❦ ~

The shapes made by tea leaves or coffee grounds
can be used for divination, too. Check the inside
of your cup next time you meet friends for coffee!

Ace of Spades: the end of a relationship . . .

Beehive: an important invitation . . .

Bottle: temptation.

Carrot: there are opportunities on the way.

Chair: if empty then someone will leave your life, if occupied then a new person will enter your life.

Clock: time is running out. Be decisive!

Deer: you will meet a timid person who could become a cherished friend.

Egg: a new beginning . . .

Face: an attractive stranger coming into your life.

Grapes: it's time to celebrate!

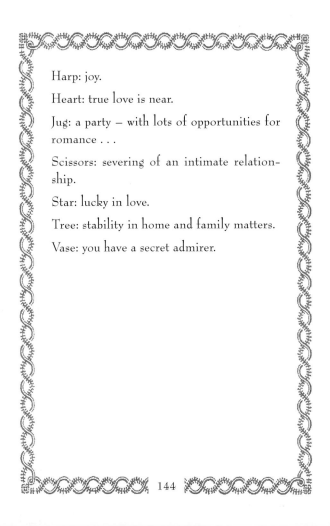

Harp: joy.

Heart: true love is near.

Jug: a party – with lots of opportunities for romance . . .

Scissors: severing of an intimate relationship.

Star: lucky in love.

Tree: stability in home and family matters.

Vase: you have a secret admirer.

SPELLS, CHARMS AND TALISMANS

~∘⚬∘~

LOVE ON THE CARDS

~

The Tarot is most usually used for divination, but it may also be used as a charm to attract love. It's not necessary to have any great knowledge of the Tarot to make such charms work, but it is useful to be familiar with the most appropriate cards for the purpose (as detailed in the next pages).

The simplest way to use the Tarot as a charm is to decide which card(s) best reflect your wishes, place it on a table before a candle (if you are using more than one card, lean them against each other to make an upright triangle), and light the candle for half an hour each evening for a week. Stay in the room, play some favorite music, daydream about what you want to happen — and later, try to remember your dreams . . .

When choosing the color of the candle,

you might like to bear in mind the following:

Red – for the new (new romance, new beginnings), and for extra will power!
Blue – for emotional encounters.
Green – for physical encounters.
Purple – for wisdom and sensuality.
White – for intellectual encounters. White can also be used as an all-purpose color, especially when you are trying to change an unpleasant or stressful situation.
Black – for strength and protection.

For example, your current relationship, with a calm, sensitive young person, is happy, but has become a little routine, and you'd like to bring a little excitement into your romance. Choose either the Princess or Prince of Cups, depending on whether your lover is female or male, and Card 17 (the Star), to represent broader horizons and new experiences. Lean the cards together in front of a red candle, and contemplate the future.

Alternatively, if you are stuck in a repressive or unhappy affair (for example with an insensitive, intolerant man who criticizes everything you do) and you want to escape, place the upended King of Wands – to represent the individual – Card 18 (the Moon) – to represent the situation – and Card 19 (the Sun) – symbolizing the happiness you hope to achieve by leaving – in a triangle before a white candle. Imagine yourself walking away and never coming back.

The Major Arcana

Card 0 – the Fool This card represents the unconventional, a new way of life, and freedom from inhibitions. It may symbolize either a person with these qualities or the qualities themselves.

Card 1 – the Magician This card symbolizes confidence, virility and creative energy. It may represent either a person with these qualities or the qualities themselves.

Card 2 – the Priestess This card represents spiritual wisdom, celibacy and inner guidance. It can represent either a person with these qualities or the qualities themselves.

Card 3 – the Empress This card symbolizes fertility, maternal love, emotional stability and fulfillment. It may represent either a person with these qualities or the qualities themselves.

Card 4 – the Emperor This card represents responsibility, authority, conventional thought and behavior, and discipline. It may symbolize either a person with these qualities or the qualities themselves.

Card 6 – the Lovers For the purposes of a Tarot charm, this card may be seen as representing a close and loving relationship, or marriage, if placed the right way up: alternatively, if it is upside down, it may be taken to mean temptation and a difficult choice in the near future.

Card 17 – the Star This card indicates a broadening of your horizons and new experiences to come.

Card 18 – the Moon This card represents an awkward situation, one which you need to resolve by yourself. It also stresses the importance of listening to your intuitions and dreams.

Card 19 – the Sun This card symbolizes

contentment, optimism, light-heartedness and joy.

Card 21 – the World This card symbolizes a successful outcome of your endeavors.

The Minor Arcana – the Court Cards

~

Use these cards to represent either the person in your life, or the person you would like to be in your life!

Please note: there will be occasions when a physically young person will act like a mature one, and when a physically mature person will act like a giddy youngster. There will also be times when a man will display the characteristics of one of the "female" cards (and vice versa). In these instances, choose the most appropriate card according to your knowledge of the individual(s) involved. ("Negative" in the following pages indicates an upside-down card.)

Wands

The Princess (or Page)
Positive – a young woman, lively, sociable, and trustworthy; possibly new to the joys of romance.

Negative — an irresponsible, shallow, irritating young woman, full of her own importance. One who brags about her love life but is actually quite inexperienced.

The Prince (or Knight)

Positive — an unpredictable, energetic and generous young man; an exciting lover.

Negative — unreliable, reckless, fickle and too quick to jump to conclusions. Keen on one-night stands . . .

The Queen

Positive — a mature woman, competent, versatile, sympathetic, passionate and independent in love.

Negative — interfering, overly protective, selfish. Often prudish and disapproving of the sexual freedom of others — possibly because of her own sexual frustration.

The King

Positive — a mature man, confident, accom-

plished, optimistic, diplomatic: in love,
receptive, understanding, witty and affectionate.

Negative – a critical, intolerant man, insensitive to the needs of other people. Often a
misogynist (most often because he is afraid
of women).

Cups

The Princess (or Page)

Positive – a thoughtful, studious, quiet and
gentle young woman, often very artistic. Very
sensitive towards a lover's needs and desires.

Negative – lazy, trivial and lacking in self-
discipline. In romance, frivolous and fun at
the time, but too flirtatious to stay with one
lover for long.

The Prince (or Knight)

Positive – a calm, imaginative young man,
easily bored and a little too easily swayed by
others' opinions. A romantic, who often
idealizes love.

Negative – weak-willed, deceitful and not to be trusted. He may use others to further his own ends.

The Queen

Positive – a mature woman, mysterious, intelligent, empathic and with profound emotional and spiritual depths. A considerate lover, with an allure many find irresistible.

Negative – charming, attractive, but nevertheless extremely vain and very selfish. Easily flattered and unlikely to remain faithful.

The King

Positive – a mature man, cultured, sophisticated, dignified and reserved. Uneasy with his own emotions, he may have a low libido and be unwilling to show affection openly.

Negative – an elegant schemer, self-centered and willfully blind to the needs of others – in his love life as much as in his public life.

Swords

The Princess (or Page)

Positive – a cautious young woman, quick-witted, far-sighted and decisive. As a lover, she make take some winning, but will be an excellent, honest and trustworthy partner.

Negative – defensive, devious and hypocritical. Romance with such an individual may leave you open to scandal or blackmail.

The Prince (or Knight)

Positive – a practical young man, forceful and resolute. In love, he lacks tenderness, and may be gauche – but is nevertheless good-hearted and honest.

Negative – aggressive, impulsive, impatient. As a lover, he is often a bully, and may resort to physical violence to get his own way.

The Queen

Traditionally, this card symbolizes a widow or a solitary woman who has suffered great sorrow and loss in her life.

Positive – a strong-willed, mature woman of great resilience and resourcefulness. She may prove extremely unwilling to be drawn into a romance.

Negative – a domineering, demanding woman, unscrupulous and embittered. She tends towards destructive relationships, and may be generally hostile.

The King

Positive – an ambitious, assertive, independent mature man. He may be unemotional, even harsh, in his relationships – and is, unfortunately, unlikely to change . . .

Negative – exploitative, capable of being extremely nasty if he doesn't get his own way. Often a tyrant in personal relationships, given to little acts of sadism that, cumulatively, can crush a kinder soul. Best avoided.

Discs

The Princess (or Page)

Positive – a sensible, methodical young woman, who likes routine and stability in her life. In romance, slow to let you know how she feels but capable of deep passion and intense loyalty.

Negative – jealous, dull, stolid, and materialistic. As a lover, she is often pompous and narrow-minded.

The Prince

Positive – a pragmatic, well meaning, but perhaps rather slow young man – modest and very aware of his own limitations, but basically unambitious. In love, he is kindly, faithful and warm, and provides security.

Negative – a sad figure, holding on to what used to work in the past because he's afraid of seeming useless or hopelessly out of date – while at the same time being unwilling to change . . . In love, he's dull and boring and may be clingy.

The Queen

Positive – an affectionate, sensuous mature women, happy with herself, her life and her sexuality. This woman will enjoy dressing in sexy clothing and playing erotic games. (She also sees having children as an essential part of her nature – so be warned!)

Negative – pretentious, materialistic and very concerned with appearances. In love, she may nag a lot, and moan about how old/fat/ugly she is . . .

The King

Positive – a successful, hard-working and secure mature man, happy in his achievements and generous with his time and affection. In love he is sensual, and truly likes and respects women for themselves.

Negative – something of a miser: often quite wealthy (and not always through legal or ethical means) but too materialistic to truly enjoy the fruits of his success. Romantically, he is usually crude, clumsy and insensitive, seeing sex as an end in itself: the idea of love is completely lost on him.

Afterword

~

If you don't have access to a Tarot pack, you can use an ordinary pack of playing cards. Substitute Clubs for Wands, Hearts for Cups, Spades for Swords, and Diamonds for Discs: use the Jack of the appropriate suit as both the Princess and the Prince (you could use a small symbol, or a piece of blue or pink ribbon, to indicate whether the individual in mind is male or female). Without the Major Arcana, you will need to have a clear idea of your desired outcome as it will be necessary to concentrate your will when lighting the candle. Meditating for a few minutes will also help focus the charm.

MAGIC SQUARES

~❦~

The Holy Magic of Abra-Melin the Mage is a fifteenth-century Grimoire, or spell book, which gives detailed instructions on how anyone who is pure of spirit can contact their guardian angel. At the climax of a 6-month ritual the magician is also introduced to a hierarchy of lower spirits who could undertake a wide range of mundane tasks.

The Grimoire provides a series of magic squares, each of which gives the ability to conjure a spirit to perform a particular task. Many of these tasks involve furthering the pursuit of love . . .

Incidentally, although modern magic squares are usually composed of numbers, ancient magicians believed that numerals and letters possess similar magical properties. The letters of the Hebrew alphabet – in which these squares were originally written – were each assigned a numerical value.

All of these squares may be used – in a suitably emotionally charged, romantic atmosphere – directly from these pages. On the other hand, you may choose to strengthen their effectiveness (particularly the square of DISAKAR) by drawing them yourself. Draw them using black ink on thin white card, on Sunday as soon after dawn as practical. They may then be used at any time.

Their effects may last a lifetime, but (we are told) their magical influence only actively operates for about a week, so periodically repeating the spell is recommended if the desired goal is not attained immediately!

CEDIDAH

This magic square reveals the secrets of the heart, and is particularly useful to discover if a certain person cherishes any fondness for you.

Simply touch the square and name aloud the person whose secrets you wish to know. A spirit will speak in your ear, revealing to you exactly who the person loves (if anyone) and describing the full extent of their feelings.

The letters of the three horizontal lines are thought to relate to love, liberty, and delight respectively.

C	E	D	I	D	A	H
E						
D						
I						
D	E	R	A	R	I	D
A						
H	A	D	I	D	E	C

DODIM

This square is particularly powerful in increasing the love between spouses.

Simply by touching the square and naming your spouse, the spirits that answer your summons will begin to strengthen the bond of love between you both. This is especially useful if you expect to feel an emotional strain – perhaps while moving house, during a holiday, taking exams or at some other trying time.

The spell is also effective for other people, when you should name both parties of the couple.

The word is supposed to mean love, rapture, and pleasure.

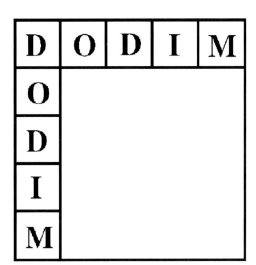

D	O	D	I	M
O				
D				
I				
M				

RAIAH

This square kindles a warm affection between people.

Touch the square and name the person whom you seek to attract in a romantic sense. The Grimoire recommends, if at all possible, that you touch the subject of your interest with the square – preferably on bare skin.

You can also use this square to stimulate and increase love between other people – simply name them both.

The first line translates as a female companion, while the meanings of the other two have been lost in the distant past.

R	A	I	A	H
A				
I	G	O	G	I
A				
H	A	I	A	H

169

IALDAH

This square builds strong bonds of friendship between people, the sort of friendship that can lead to romance and develop into love.

Touching the square and naming the person to whom you wish to become allied is all that is necessary.

You may also use this square to influence a couple to grow closer in affection; simply name them both while touching the square.

The Grimoire recommends that, if it is possible, you try to touch the subject/s of your interest with the square – preferably on bare skin.

I	A	L	D	A	H
A	Q	O	R	I	A
L	O	Q	I	R	E
D	R	I	I	D	E
A	I	R	D	R	O
H	A	F	E	O	N

DISAKAR

This square is used to cultivate youthfulness in mind, body and spirit.

There is no doubt that the young-at-heart are commonly judged to be more attractive than those who have been prematurely aged by the rigors of life. It is to rediscover that endearing sense of wonder in the simple things of life, and to regain the vigor to gallantly meet the challenges that life puts our way, that this square is best employed.

The effect is traditionally achieved by taking up the symbol with the left hand, and stroking it gently across your face (a practice that may be easily incorporated into your morning routine).

The word on the topmost horizontal line means "youthful."

D	I	S	A	K	A	R
I	R	O	Q			
S				Q		
A	Q					
K	U	Q				
A						
R						

CRYSTAL TALISMANS FOR LOVERS

~

Shakespeare said, "The course of true love never did run smooth . . ." and very often it's true. However, there are ways you can ease its progress. Try some of the following ideas and see what happens!

Shyness

~

It happens to nearly everyone. You've met someone to whom you are strongly attracted – but every time you find yourself in his/her presence you freeze up!

Take a good-sized piece of tiger's eye (for courage) and citrine (for eloquence). Grip them tightly between your hands, holding them at the level of your heart. Close your eyes, imagine the other person, and repeat to yourself, three times:

"I charge you, citrine and tiger's eye, to give me the courage to speak to [name], that I may discover his/her feeling for me."

Carry the stones with you whenever you know you will be in the other's presence, and to give the talismans extra energy, handle them while imagining his/her face. (You might find it helpful to sleep with the stones under your pillow, too.) If you prefer — and especially if shyness is a constant feature in your dealings with others — you could always wear the stones as jewelry: both gems are often found as rings or earrings.

Choosing

~

Making the right choice in romantic matters can be very difficult. How do you choose between several equally attractive people – especially if you are young and inexperienced?

To some extent, you need to trust your feelings, and any messages your subconscious – which normally has a good handle on what's what where people are concerned – might give you. However, you can give this a helping hand with a clear quartz double terminated crystal. While it can't make the choices for you, it can, with a little luck, help to steer you in the right direction.

You need to get to know your crystal. Study and explore it, until you know every flaw, facet and inclusion. Then sleep with it under your pillow – or in your hand – for five nights, writing down your dreams each morning.

Finally, take the crystal to a river or lake, and walk slowly along the bank. When you reach a spot that seems particularly pleasant, or interesting, stop for a while and look around you. Hold the crystal in your hand and gaze into it, repeating:

"Be with me in my choosing:

May your calm strength pass into me, that I may not err."

Your can repeat this formula whenever you need to. It's also a good idea to carry the crystal with you at all times.

Passion

∼

The first throes of love are usually a time when the rest of the world fades into insignificance and all that matters is your beloved – and what you do together . . . Fortunately, those in love are usually regarded with a smile and allowed a little more license than would otherwise be the case: these days, even employers are beginning to realize that happy workers are efficient workers!

However, to help you have the energy to cope both with your day-to-day life and the excitement of romance, try carrying a carnelian or a piece of red jasper. Keep it with you when you and your beloved are together, and take a moment or two to focus that glorious feeling of rapture and power into the stone.

Keep the stone with you in your normal

daily life and work, and handle it every time you feel your concentration slipping. Remind yourself that the sooner you finish your appointed tasks, the sooner you can be together again: use the stone as a talisman to boost your performance in all things!

Frivolity

~

Sometimes a new relationship can be a little too heavy, shutting out the rest of the world in favor of an intense, exclusive one-to-one, often centered on the bedroom. While this is fine in its place, it also means missing out on a lot of fun if it becomes a habit.

Buy yourself and your lover a piece of amethyst each (ones with rainbows are most effective – and probably the least expensive) – and then take them with you to a seriously silly place! Fun-fairs, carnivals, The Rocky Horror Show, a burlesque performance – whatever feels most appealing, as long as it is loud, manic and fun. Join in the spirit of the occasion: wear silly hats or noses, try a ride you've never tried before, throw peanuts at the actors (as long as you won't be thrown out), join in the choruses of the songs – just do something daft you'd never normally dream of doing. It's surprising how much of a release this can provide, and if nothing else, you'll feel closer from doing something silly together.

Try to channel the fun and frivolity of the experience into the crystals, so that handling them will bring back a sense of the excitement and pleasure you enjoyed together. Any time you feel things are becoming too oppressive, take your crystals for a day out (drag your partner along too!) and see if you can recapture that magic . . .

Tenderness

~

Hopefully, tender loving care will never be absent from your relationship. However, it does sometimes happen that your partner is less attentive and considerate than you'd like. Depending on the sort of person they are, you can make your point by reasoning with them, sulking loudly, flirting with everyone in sight, or going on strike . . .

However you choose to handle the situation, having a small crystal as a talisman may help. Choose moonstone (if you're female) or milky quartz (if you're male), clean the stone well and immerse it in a glass of mineral water. Leave the glass on your windowsill for a couple of hours (preferably in moonlight, and during the waxing moon is best). Take the stone from the water and hold it in your cupped hands, concentrating on the treatment you'd like from your partner: then consider what you could do for them in return. Try to think yourself inside your partner's mind, seeing things from their point of view. After all, your own behavior may not be improving the situation!

Drink the water, all the while thinking loving thoughts toward your partner. Then hold the stone while you talk to them about your feelings – try to remain calm and non-accusatory. If you like, you could give them the crystal as a gift, but be sure they understand that it represents your wish for tenderness in the relationship.

Energy

～

Love affairs can really take their toll – of your time, your emotions, and your energy! If you're finding everything all just a bit too tiring to be fun anymore, try the following.

Run a deep, warm bath, adding pine-scented bath foam or bath salts. Dim the lights (or light a couple of deep green candles), play some favorite music (light classical or New Age is best), and relax in the water. Have a glass of wine, if you like, and a bowl of strawberries would also be appropriate. Most importantly, have to hand a piece of malachite – a heart-shaped pendant would be ideal.

As you soak, hold the stone before you and watch the light play over its banding. Repeat to yourself (and the stone):

"You are the green and growing things of the earth. You are the spring, the patient cycle of the seasons. Grant me to share in your vitality, your strength, your power."

Afterwards, carrying the malachite with you, take a leisurely walk somewhere green — a wood, a park, even your yard. Listen to the sounds, smell the air, feel the air on your skin. Be aware of the multitude of tiny sensations around you, and feel yourself a part of them, plugged in to the energy of nature. Carrying or wearing the stone can help you to generate that feeling any time you need a boost.

Stamina

~

There are times — bad patches, disappointments, financial or emotional troubles — when you simply need to be able to hang on and get through, somehow. Your own inner strength will pull you through most things, but sometimes you need a little extra boost.

Hematite — that beautiful, heavy, silvery black stone — is ideal as a talisman for such situations: not only does it, traditionally, deflect negativity, but it is also a very protective stone. If everything is going wrong in your love-life, take time out and obtain a large piece of hematite, and retire to a very solitary place (your own room if that's all that is available, although somewhere out of doors would be better).

Grip the stone tightly, focusing all your anxiety and uncertainty onto its shining surface — and imagine the stone shrugging off the problems with sublime confidence! Consider the good things in your life, then think about the ways you can improve — or, if there is no other option, escape from — the current situation.

It's very unlikely that you'll find an immediate solution, but at least you will have taken the first steps to resolving the problems — calm consideration of all the options open to you. Carry the hematite with you and handle it frequently, letting its cool solidity echo in your own actions, and borrowing its strength as you learn to deal with the unpleasant things of life!

Understanding

~

Understanding, forgiveness, acceptance, tolerance . . . These are very often incredibly difficult things to feel, especially if you're feeling a little insecure and uncertain in yourself. Nevertheless they are essential if your relationship is to flourish — and that means you have to feel them about yourself as well as your partner.

It's often hard to forgive, and accept, ourselves as fallible humans, making mistakes and getting things wrong, especially when we're in love and want everything to be perfect.

Find a piece of turquoise — there's so much turquoise jewelry available you should be able to find something that appeals to you, but if not, buy (or be given) the raw material. As well as being a traditional spiritual stone, turquoise can, with concentration, allow you to delve into your own mind . . .

Ideally, find somewhere high – a hillside, clifftop, the top floor of a high rise, the place matters less than the view. Compare the color of your stone to the sky; watch the clouds; feel your spirit rising above the earth, and soaring upwards . . .

From far above, human concerns seem small and insignificant – or at least more in proportion! It's a lot easier to forgive yourself, and those you love, for foibles, mistakes and imperfections when you can fly high above them.

Of course, you need to come back to earth eventually, but bring your new perspective – and the turquoise that embodies it – back with you. Not an easy operation, but it will make you a far wiser, and far more attractive, individual!

Letting Go

~

Sometimes, no matter how hard you've worked at a relationship, or how much you want it to continue, the other person is no longer in love with you and wants to be set free. You could fight for them to stay, of course, but it's wiser, kinder, and ultimately healthier, to let them go.

However, this is often easier said than done, especially if you still love him/her. To make things a little less difficult, find a piece of amazonite or sodalite (or both), and keep them with you through the difficult time. They are both "feel good" stones, comforting to handle and attractive to look at; their colors are soothing and they may help you to feel a little more optimistic about life in general.

It's important, in such a situation, that you don't lose your sense of your own worth.

This relationship may not have been successful, but there's no reason why the next one should go the same way, especially if you can learn from your mistakes. Keep the stone(s) with you to remind you that things aren't as gloomy as they might appear.

Escape

~

Sometimes you yourself are the one who wants to be set free, especially from a restrictive or possessive partner (if he/she is also abusive or violent, it would be far better to get professional help rather than rely on talismans or books, no matter how well-meaning). Such a move takes will power, determination and self-confidence: help the process along with serpentine, snowflake obsidian, or moss agate. Wearing the stone as jewelry is a good idea in this situation – that way you can keep it with you at all times – but if this isn't possible, try to find a comfortably large piece to carry with you. A "worry egg" would be highly appropriate; the egg shape represents undiscovered potential and new life.

As forcefully as you can, imagine yourself leading a different life, one that doesn't include the partner you're trying to leave, while holding the stone tightly. Will yourself to be strong, and not to let your lover induce you to stay. Convince yourself of your determination to start over by yourself, regardless of what he/she says. Then have the stone with you during what is bound to be an awkward confrontation . . .

Afterwards, handle the stone as much as you need to un-stress yourself – then start thinking about all the new experiences and people that will come your way!

THE PERFUMED LOVER

~

The fragrance you choose to use (as perfume, after-shave, body lotion etc.) can say a great deal about you: the human sense of smell may not be as acute as that of our canine companions, but aromas – both pleasant and unpleasant – produce a strong emotional response. It's worth while thinking about the sort of fragrance connected with the image you wish to project – it's an important part of weaving love magic!

It's a good idea to take along an absolutely honest friend when choosing a personal fragrance. Human skin varies widely in its responses to the chemicals in perfumes, colognes, etc., and something that smells sublime on someone else might smell absolutely vile on you!

Fragrances

∾

Women are far better provided for than men when it comes to perfumes, but with a bit of imagination it is quite possible to find comparable fragrances for the male of the species!

Sweet and old-fashioned To summon up images of happy contentment in a little cottage in the country, try floral scents – rose, violet, honeysuckle and jasmine.

Lively and sporty To impress your lover with your keenness for the active life, experiment with fresh, sharp perfumes that smell like a breath of fresh air!

Independent and outdoor loving Woody and outdoor scents – pine, sandalwood and grass – express your love for long country walks and sharing a mug of soup over the campfire.

Cool and sophisticated Spicy or citrus-based perfumes – lemon, bergamot or ginger – can make you appear something of a challenge, so use with care!

Sensual and exciting Warm, "musky" scents, the sort that make your lover want to wrap you in satin and take you somewhere private!

Mysterious and exotic Try myrrh or patchouli based scents, fragrances that remind your lover of faraway countries, the richness of oriental palaces, the glamor of unknown and unexplored places . . .

Natural You could always be daring and try not wearing any perfume at all! Use unperfumed soap, forego heavily scented deodorant, and let your own natural fragrance come through. You might be pleasantly surprised at the response from your partner.

THE LESSER KEY OF SOLOMON

~

Also called the *Lemegeton*, this ancient magical text details how to call forth powerful spirits and set them to work on your behalf. It lists 72 spirits willing and able to grant humanity their services, and catalogues their individual strengths, abilities and appearances.

The idea of "conjuring spirits" may sound strange in this day and age, but in effect the procedure was the medieval equivalent of getting in touch with deeply buried elements of yourself (or contacting the collective unconscious, if you prefer). By performing the following rituals, you are really doing nothing more than reaching into your own psyche – but if you are the least bit uneasy with the thought of invoking such forces, or performing these rites, then please give them a miss! (You can still carry or wear the symbols as talismans.) However, for the more adventurous amongst you, find a time and place where you won't be disturbed, read through the following pages, and see what results . . .

Many of the spirits profess to bring love to the ardent seeker but, as some of them also had the reputation of mischievously stirring up strife between people, only four are given here.

The procedure for calling them forth from the invisible realms where they dwell is fairly straightforward (although in the original Key it is dressed up in archaic formulae and cryptic rigmarole). It may readily be translated as nothing more than the customary hospitality that you would offer to an employee with whom you wish to discuss a project dear to your heart.

First, construct the pendant with the

symbol of the spirit with which you wish to communicate (either as detailed in each section below, or simply photocopied directly from these pages). Keep it in a safe place, carefully wrapped (cotton of the appropriate color is ideal) to prevent you unexpectedly gazing on it and mentally calling upon the spirit without proper preparation!

Then you need arrange the meeting for a mutually convenient time – for our purpose the three days of the full moon are perfect.

Next, you, the magician, must prepare for the spirit's visit by attending to your personal hygiene, bathing and clearing your mind of distractions. Once you're certain of your mental readiness, like any good business host you should ensure that the interview room is clean and that your desk is tidy.

You may like to light candles and incense. It may be useful to imagine yourself in the middle of a large circle that no spirit can enter without being invited – a little like sitting on the boss's side of the desk! (Some people like to trace the edge of this barrier with a thin scattering of salt.)

When you invite the employee in it is polite to offer him a seat, so the magician should prepare a small equal-sided triangle in which the spirit can conveniently rest while you discuss your needs. This triangle, which need only be six inches across, may be drawn on a piece of paper and placed on the floor – outside of the circle.

Then you simply call the spirit to come to you and make itself comfortable in the triangle. Always call the spirit by name. Sometimes, the *Lemegeton* says, the spirits are right there waiting to be called, but other times they may already be engaged on other business, and you may need to be patient and call repeatedly, and with authority, before they answer your summons.

Once you feel the spirit is with you,

present your ideas to it. State your desires simply, briefly, and in as matter-of-fact a way as you can under the circumstances. (The spirit needs the instructions to be perfectly clear — you cannot expect it to have any prior knowledge about you or your intentions, or even to know anything about the person you are wooing!)

This is where good preparation really pays off — the time you spent earlier, clearing and focusing your mind on what you are doing, should prevent you from making any foolish mistakes. If you are worried you might forget to mention something, then write yourself a script and simply read it to the spirit!

Once the spirit has been briefed you should thank it for its time and attention — but don't offer any thanks or debt of gratitude for the tasks that it has yet to perform. After all, these spirits are subservient to your will and are duty bound to honor your demands. As you bid the spirit goodbye you may mention that you would like it to return promptly if you call again.

Sytry

This spirit has just one function – to enflame men and women with lust and desire for each other!

It is traditionally envisaged as a handsome prince – who can also appear with wings of a griffin and the noble head of a leopard or other wild animal. It delights in nakedness, and can bring you visions of anyone, man or woman, to dance lasciviously before your gaze.

Its symbol should be written in blue ink on blue card (or engraved on a disc of tin), and worn on a blue ribbon to rest over your heart. If the rest of the ritual equipment is blue then so much the better. The best time to summon Sytry is Thursday (the hour isn't important).

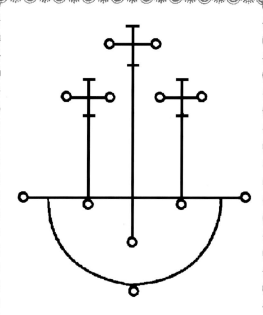

Sallos

This spirit inspires love between men and women.

Envisage Sallos as a handsome duke in the armor of a gallant soldier – riding on the back of a crocodile!

Despite its dramatic appearance, it is a peaceful spirit, and may be called upon to brings hearts together in unity and harmony.

Its symbol should be written in green ink on green card (or engraved on a disc of copper), and worn on a green ribbon to rest over your heart. If the rest of the ritual equipment is green then so much the better. The best time to summon Sallos is between dawn and noon on Friday.

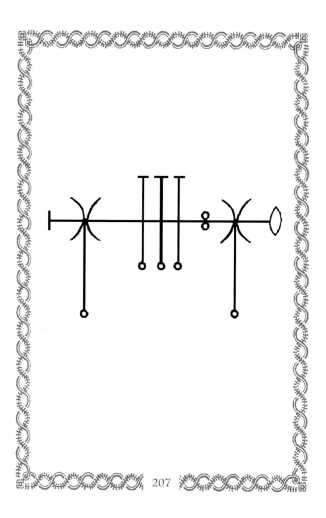

Vual

This spirit is particularly adept at attracting women to love you, but it can also promote a close, even intimate, friendship between people irrespective of their sex.

Imagine Vual as a mighty duke, appearing as a muscular Egyptian (or even at first as a dromedary). It can also be called upon to answer any questions about things past, present or to come, especially where they relate to romance.

Its symbol should be written in green ink on green card (or engraved on a disc of copper), and worn on a green ribbon to rest over your heart. If the rest of the ritual equipment is green then so much the better. The best time to summon Vual is between dawn and noon on Friday.

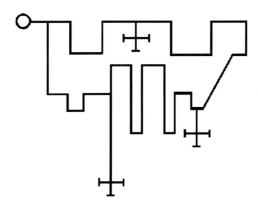

Dantalian

This spirit inspires the highest form of romantic – even spiritual – love.

Traditionally seen as a mighty duke, Dantalian has a strange appearance – its face can appear in the likeness of any man or woman. If you can, imagine its countenance continually changing, revealing a myriad different faces (this spirit can be seen as symbolizing both all the people you have ever met, and all the different facets of your own personality).

The love it brings is such that each party not only knows what the other is thinking and feeling when they are together, but is as keenly aware of the other's wellbeing despite being separated by half the world!

Its symbol should be written in green ink on green card (or engraved on a disc of copper), and worn on a green ribbon to rest over your heart. If the rest of the ritual equipment is green then so much the better. The best time to summon Dantalian is between dawn and noon on Friday.

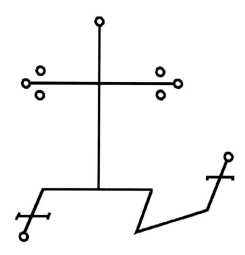

THE LOVING YEAR

212

BELTAIN (MAY DAY)

~

Beltain is the greatest fertility festival of the year! Represented by the union of Cernunnos (the Lord of Nature) with the Earth Goddess, it is a day for feasting, fun and romance.

Maypoles are still set up in many places: these represent masculine energy, and the traditional dance around them symbolizes the irresistible energy of Life itself.

Women, both young and old, should make a point of going out just before dawn to wash their faces in morning dew to make themselves beautiful (in spirit if not in body!) – if it can be gathered from under an oak or hawthorn tree, so much the better:

> "The lass who at the break of day
> Goes abroad on the first of May

To wash in dew from the hawthorn tree
Will ever after lovely be."

Speak the name of the person whose affection you wish to attract while doing so, saying

"[name] – my wish upon this special day is that my lover you may be".

An old custom also says that if you wash your feet in dew from the marigold flower, you will be able to understand the language of birds – and perhaps give truth to the saying "a little bird told me . . ."

Those wishing to attract a lover should wear oak or hawthorn leaves, primroses, or a daisy chain. Women wishing to become pregnant should touch an apple or cherry tree – or, even better, join in the dance around a Maypole!

MIDSUMMER SOLSTICE

~

Midsummer Eve is the best time in the year for love magic. Ideally, you should stay up all night to watch the sunrise – preferably in the company of your beloved: doing so should ensure that your love will stay fresh and true for another year! However, if you do fall asleep, try to remember your dreams: it is said that midsummer dreams will always come true (no mention is made of nightmares, so we can safely assume that they will not . . .).

If you don't have a partner, go out before dawn to a hill or high place from which you can watch the sunrise. Take with you a piece of rose quartz and/or malachite (if you have any emerald or peridot jewelry, make a point of wearing it), a small bottle of mead or white wine, and two red roses, cowslip, yarrow, clover or daisies – if possible, pick the flowers on your way. Stand facing the rising sun, hold the stones and flowers in front of you, and say:

"I greet you [Sol/Ra/Apollo/Lugh – use your preferred name for the sun] on this most special morning. May love fill my life as your light fills the world."

Pour a few drops of the mead or wine onto the ground, drink a little yourself, and on your return eat a meal of wholegrain bread and fresh oranges to complete the spell!

LUGHNASADH

~

Lughnasadh (pronounced LOO nah sah – August 1) is the festival of the first fruits of the year's harvest. This is an ideal time for those who have been partners for some time (years rather than months!) to reaffirm their love for each other, and weave a little magic to ensure that love continues for years to come.

Wearing the appropriate colors (red for the male, green for the female) and flowers (oak leaves or heather for the male, poppies or sunflower for the female), you should both go into the countryside: if you can get access to a wheatfield, so much the better, but anywhere food is grown is fine – a farm, vineyard, orchard, even your own vegetable patch: whatever is most convenient. Take along a small symbolic gift for each other. If it should be raining, take a red, green or rainbow-colored umbrella with you!

Find a secluded spot in your chosen location, kneel on the ground facing each other (if it's muddy, stand facing each other instead), exchange gifts, hold hands, and say to each other:

"I thank you for your trust, your friendship and your affection. In this place, on the good Earth, I celebrate our love: may it grow and flourish, bright and nourishing as the harvest."

Finish with a hearty hug and a kiss (if the weather is fine and the place private enough, you could take this further . . .).

HARVEST

~

The Autumn Equinox celebrates the full-
ness of the year's harvest. It's a special time
for older lovers and partners, especially if
they have children. To keep the flame of
family love alive, organize a special meal.

Decorate the table with acorns,
pinecones, corn dollies or kirn babies,
poppies and nuts (especially hazel, which is
reputed to endow the eater with wisdom);
light straw-colored or dark green candles;
and ensure the meal includes bread, a lot of
different root vegetables, and blackberries.
When all the family have assembled, hold
hands around the table and say:

"[Demeter/Gaia/Great Mother – use any
deity name that seems most suitable to you]
we give you thanks for all the good things
you have given us: the food we eat, the life

we enjoy, the love we share. Teach us to treat you with respect and love throughout the coming year. We ask your blessing on us all."

Save a little of the food and drink (no more than will fit on a small saucer) and at the end of the meal, bury it in the ground — in your yard if you have one, or in a favorite spot out of doors. This symbolic gift acts as a thanksgiving offering to the nurturing Earth, affirming your appreciation for her bounty.

SAMHAIN

~

Samhain (pronounced "SAH wen": the night of October 31/November 1) is the ancient Celtic New Year. It marks the start of the Dark Year: at this time the barriers between the human and supernatural worlds grow thin, allowing spirits to pass between the two. It's considered very unlucky to refuse hospitality to strangers, in case they are actually visitors from the otherworld, or the spirits of ancestors come back to check that all is well – for the sake of your personal safety, it's perfectly all right to be hospitable outside your home rather than inviting strangers in! Samhain is the ideal time of year for divination and making wishes . . .

Samhain is known as the Feast of Apples, and any spells you perform at this time of year should involve this magical fruit. At midnight, sit before a mirror with a lighted candle at each side, and brush your hair while eating an apple: the face of your future partner may appear reflected in the glass, looking over your shoulder. Alternatively, hold an apple and stand in front of the mirror; make a wish, then eat the apple – this should ensure it comes true. (Rather more messily, you could also try taking the seeds from an apple, giving each the name of a potential lover, and sticking them onto your cheeks. The last one to fall off is the most suitable choice for you!)

YULE

~

The Midwinter Solstice. Yule celebrates the rebirth of the sun – from this day the nights get shorter and the days longer.

Yule is a very special time, full of hope for the year to come. Gifts are exchanged, parties enjoyed, and most of us indulge in rich food, drink and festivities. The atmosphere of abundant goodwill and fellowship at this time of year makes it ideal for approaching the person you've had your eye on and inviting them out, to a party, movie, or just for a walk on a crisp and starry night . . .

Try cutting an apple in half vertically, and count the seeds in each half. If there is an equal number, a romance is forecast for the very near future: however, if one of the seeds has been cut, the relationship will have stormy patches.

Holly and mistletoe are traditional Yuletide plants: the red berries of the holly represent the blood of the Earth Goddess, while the white berries of the mistletoe symbolize the seed of the Sun God (kissing under the mistletoe was originally a fertility charm!) Holly is a luck-bringer, and mistletoe can act as a charm to ensure your love remains ever-true: kiss your lover under a sprig while repeating, mentally,

"[name], be ever mine."

It would be wise, however, to be certain you wish to spend your life with him or her before trying this spell!

IMBOLC

~

Imbolc (February 1) is often the very coldest time of the year, and Imbolc celebrates the White Lady, the earth slowly awakening into spring. Snowdrops, those lovely little flowers that symbolize "Hope," are just about the only things in flower in colder northern climes, and so have come to represent the optimism of this season.

Imbolc is a good time to practice a little candle-magic. Take a white candle for each of your potential lovers and lightly carve each of their names into the wax — it's best to use quite small candles for this, since ideally you will watch over them until they have all burned out. Depending on the number of candles, position them in a line or a circle, with one pink or blue candle in the middle (or use silver or gold; this candle represents you, and can be in your favorite color if you prefer). You will need to decide, in advance, what sign you wish to reveal your ideal choice: it could be the first candle to burn down or go out, or the last candle to do the same.

When you have decided, light all of the candles, and sit waiting for your chosen sign to occur. (If you already have a secret preference, you could always try to extinguish, or make to burn until last, the candle for that person. Who knows, you might discover an unrecognized talent for psychokinesis!)

ST VALENTINE'S DAY

~

February 14. This festival has a close association with the lupercalia of ancient Rome, held on February 15, when the beginning of spring was celebrated with wild and orgiastic festivities! It is sacred to lovers, and the perfect time for love spells . . .

Place bay leaves under your pillow and recite –

"Let this night be good to me,
And I in dreams my true love see."

February 14 in a Leap Year was, traditionally, the time when a woman could propose marriage to her beloved. He didn't have to accept, of course – but if he refused he was supposed to buy her a pure silk gown as consolation . . .

These days, treating your loved one to a special meal, or flowers and chocolates, are more usual offerings. You could try including some of the traditional aphrodisiacs, or foods of love, in the meal: oysters, asparagus, truffles, strawberries, honey, cream-filled or chocolate confections (and worry about the diet the following day . . .).

To cast a special Valentine's day spell, take strawberries (for promises of delights to come), cherries (for lively romance), hazelnuts (for wise choices) or brazil nuts (for good luck in love): melt chocolate in a bowl over a pan of boiling water and dunk the fruit and nuts one at a time into the chocolate, making an appropriate wish as you do so. Cool the sweets on greaseproof paper, then place them in tissue in a pretty box and give them to your loved one as a gift. (You might like to make a note of how many – and which – of the wishes come true!)

EOSTRE

~

The Vernal (Spring) Equinox is a time of rejoicing that spring, with all its attendant happiness, has arrived. And of course, in Spring "a young man's (and woman's) fancy turns to love . . ."

This is the festival of Eostre, the ancient goddess of spring fertility. Hares and eggs are her symbols, and – weather permitting – this is an excellent time for loving couples to take a walk in the country (or at least the local park!) and enjoy both the general feel-good atmosphere and each other's company. If you can find some violets, so much the better – they symbolize constancy, modesty and faithfulness. Stand by the patch and indulge in a long, lingering kiss, but be careful not to crush any of the flowers!

Try a little egg magic. Take the (clean!)

rounded end of an eggshell, place in it a scrap of paper with the name of your beloved written on it. Light a yellow or light green candle and allow the wax to drip onto and over the paper until it is completely sealed in a covering of wax, but don't fill the eggshell: it must be able to float. Take it to the nearest water source and cast it carefully adrift on the water, saying with all your heart:

"[Name], as I set you free, may you choose to stay with me,

Where so ever you may roam, may I always be your home."

CAST A WICCAN SPELL . . . (TWO RITUALS TO HELP YOUR LOVE-LIFE)

~❦~

There may come a time when you feel that nothing less than a full, whole-hearted ritual will help you gain your heart's desire. The following rites utilize elemental energies and correspondences, and may act to make your dreams come true. There's certainly no harm in trying!

The rituals can be adapted to fit your own preferences for color, music, even language. It is useful, but not essential, to set aside a special place (in your yard for example, or a spare room if you have one): at the very least try to keep something – a candle or holder, some fragrance oil, perhaps a special chalice — that you use only for such rituals. Before starting, have a light meal (apples, strawberries, nectarines or peaches, grapes, and a glass of mineral water, would be ideal), and a cleansing bath of warm water with a handful of sea-salt added. You can also add fresh herbs or flowers if you prefer — lavender, rosemary, thyme, rose petals, jasmine and honeysuckle are best.

Whether you prefer to work sky-clad (nude) or clothed is entirely up to you — and possibly the law where you live! Bear in mind getting arrested isn't usually very good for your love life . . . If you're happier dressed, a loose, comfortable robe is appropriate: designing and sewing your own will make it even more special. White is the best color, as it contains all colors. Keep it for ritual use only.

It would be very useful to have a sturdy, low table on which to place candles etc. during the ritual. The aim is to engage all the senses, so try to have a music source nearby, and explore different methods of perfuming your space — joss sticks, fragrance oil, incense grains on glowing charcoal — until you find one that is best for you. It's traditional to have at hand an object to represent each of the elements: a small knife for fire, a wand or baton for air, a stone or coin for earth, and a chalice for water are the most usual, but by all means use anything that feels right to you.

Read through each ritual and make sure you have everything you need before starting.

TO FIND TRUE LOVE

~

Set aside a Friday morning, during the moon's first quarter. Beltain is the best occasion, but any time in spring would be the most beneficial; however this is less important than the day and time. Try to wear a pine-scented fragrance and have pine incense handy. Wear amber or green jewelry – emeralds, peridot, malachite and jade are ideal stones. Deep green and rose-red are the ideal colors if you're wearing ordinary clothes: if you have a robe, twist together dark green and red cord to make a loose belt.

You should have two tall candles, one green and one dark pink: if you want more candles, make sure they are the same colors but smaller. Try to have something made of copper on the table – a coin, bangle, or a piece of the raw metal – and a pot of living miniature roses. (Violets would be a second choice, or if nothing else is available a single red rose in a dark green vase, but bear in mind it's always preferable to have something alive, rather than dying, in such rituals.)

You should also have a couple of honey cakes on a pottery plate and a small bottle of mead (if mead isn't available, dessert wine, the sweeter the better, is fine).

Music is an intensely personal thing, so you'll need to make your own choice: it should be quietly thrilling to create the right atmosphere, but not too loud or stirring.

It's wise to spend a little time meditating before starting this ritual: for it to be successful you need to have some idea of exactly what true love means to you. Are you looking for a partner who will fulfill your every whim? Someone who will look after you? Someone you can look after? Or are you looking for a true partner, an equal to share the highs and lows of life with you? Once you have decided what you want, fix the thought in your mind and begin.

Pull the curtains if you're inside, to make the area dim but not gloomy. Set the incense going, start the music, and light the smaller candles if you are using them. Stand in front of the table, close your eyes and focus on your ideal of true love. Raise your arms, hands open and facing upwards, to chest height. Speaking aloud, repeat the following:

"I, [your name], stand here as a supplicant at the threshold of love.

I come here freely, my heart and my mind as open and accepting as my hands.

I wait to welcome love into my life."

Open your eyes and light the two tall candles, placing them close together on the table with the copper object between and touching them both. Gaze into the flames for a moment, then kneel or sit before the table. Close your eyes and cross your hands over your heart, saying:

"As these flames are strong and true, so will be my heart."

For a moment or two concentrate on your heartbeat, becoming aware of its quietly powerful steady rhythm. Raise your hands to cover your face, then slowly move them away until your arms are stretched out to your sides, saying:

"I will not hide from love, nor will I blind myself to its possibilities.

I will watch and wait, neither hunter nor prey, but simply and wholly MYSELF."

Open your eyes, lower your hands, and smile – really smile – and mean it. Feel happiness and a sense of anticipation, touched with wonder. You are working magic in yourself: celebrate the fact!

Sit for a few minutes, completely relaxed and in tune with yourself. When you are ready, bring your hands together, one cupped over the other, and slowly open and raise them (as though setting free a butterfly or dove). Repeat, mentally if you prefer:

"My spirit is free, my heart is free, I am free.

I am loving and worthy of love.

I am a mystery, awaiting the one who will come adventuring.

I am a fire burning steady and true in the dark places of the world.

Who knows me, has a gift indeed."

Hug yourself, as though you hold a great secret close to your heart (which is in fact now true!) Then relax for a moment: pour yourself a glass of the mead or wine, and eat the honey cakes. Remember to reserve a little of the wine and a few crumbs of the cakes for later. When you are ready, extinguish the smaller candles (leave the tall ones to burn out of their own accord) and kneel for a few minutes before the table. Close the ritual, saying:

"As I leave this quiet place, I take its mystery with me.

I will not forget, neither will I be false to myself.

For knowledge, for wisdom and the strength to use them wisely, I give thanks."

Open the curtains (open the window if it's warm enough!), and relax. Stretch out, breathe deeply, smile happily – and try looking in a mirror. Often, after this ritual, you can see a difference in your appearance: you may look happier, or there may be an added sparkle to your eyes. You may even see yourself faintly outlined in gold, a sign that your aura has been strengthened and made whole through your own efforts! You'll almost certainly notice a difference in the reactions of others toward you . . .

Remember to take the leftover wine and cake outside and offer it as a libation to the Earth. It's an ancient way of saying "thanks" that's just as relevant today as in olden times.

If you wish to use this ritual to dedicate a talisman or amulet, have it sitting on or touching the copper object, and just before closing the rite, touch the talisman, saying:

"As I carry you with me into the world, may you bring my true love to me."

Carry the talisman with you always.

There is absolutely no reason why you can't repeat this ritual as often as you like!

TO KEEP LOVE STRONG
AND TRUE

~

This ritual is designed for those in a long-term relationship, who wish to reaffirm their love and gather strength for the future. It's ideal when starting on a major new and exciting phase of your life together – after deciding to try for a first child, for example, or uprooting in order to move abroad. Ideally, the ritual should be performed with your partner, but only if you are both happy to do so.

Set aside a Sunday when you know you won't be disturbed – any time in the summer or early autumn is fine, but try to make it a sunny day. Eat something rich before beginning the ritual: paté is ideal for a light meal, or a portion of casserole in a wine or cream sauce. Wear yellow or gold colored clothing (or a gold belt if wearing a robe), and simple

gold, or gold and diamond, jewelry: a single
neck chain, ring or earring(s). Use sandalwood or patchouli perfume.

Cover the table with a rich deep blue
cover, and put a plate containing oranges,
olives, sunflowers and marigolds, juniper
berries and/or bay leaves in the center. Have
two small pieces of tiger's eye, two gold
candles in gold-colored holders, and a small
bowl of sunflower seeds and hazelnuts, to
hand. Try to use a glowing charcoal tablet
(preferably in a gold-colored metal burner)
and grains of frankincense if at all possible:
if not, a clove or cinnamon scented joss
stick will suffice.

Leave the curtains open for the sun to
shine in, and if the weather is warm enough,
open a couple of windows as well. Place red
or orange floor cushions before the table,
keep a bottle of full-bodied red wine (or
ruby port if you prefer) nearby, light the
candles, and place the tiger's eye between

them. As ever, music is a matter of personal preference, but ideally play something which makes you feel positive and happy, and/or something you and your partner consider to be "your tune."

If you are performing the ritual together, sit on the cushions facing each other and hold hands. Spend at least ten minutes gazing at each other, rediscovering each other's features — even those little lines and wrinkles you haven't noticed before! (If you are performing the ritual alone, use a good recent photograph of your partner instead.)

Still holding hands (or gazing at your partner's photograph), repeat the following (substitute your own version if you choose, but make sure that you mean what you are saying):

"As I once chose you to be my love, so I love you still.

Your presence is with me always: wherever I am, there you are too.

Your love brightens my life, and helps me stay strong.

Knowing you has brought me joy."

(Lay your palm against your partner's face, and smile.)

"For your love, for your affection and companionship,

I give you thanks.

For sharing my life and opening yours to me,

I give you thanks.

To the powers that brought us together,

I give thanks."

(Take one tiger's eye each and hold hands again — if you're alone hold one in each hand and clasp your hands together.)

"As we charge these stones with the force of our love, may we always keep the magic alive in our hearts, and in our lives."

Here add a few words to invoke the purpose of the ritual — if it's prior to conception, you could say something along the lines of: –

"Grant that we may share our love with the child that is born of that love: to protect without smothering, to be firm without harshness, and to love with wisdom and tolerance."

For a move abroad: –

"Grant us the strength and courage to grasp the future, to enjoy without regret, and to understand without prejudice. May our endeavors always be crowned with success!"

If you are reaffirming your love, and you are together, a warm, loving cuddle is probably more appropriate!

Eat some of the seeds and nuts, and at least one orange, and sip a glass of the wine or port. You could also weave some of the marigolds into each other's hair for a light-hearted touch. If the aim of the ritual is to try for a child – or to strengthen your feelings for each other – now is a good time to disappear to the bedroom (or rearrange the floor cushions and stay where you are!) Make sure you keep the stones with you, and if you're leaving the room extinguish the candles first, for safety.

To close the rite, place the tiger's eye on the table and kneel side by side facing it. Raise your hands, palms upwards, and repeat: —

"For each other, for love, and for all the good things in life, we give thanks."

Keep one of the stones safe, as a talisman, and bury the other in a favorite place out of doors (remember to scatter a few seeds and a drop or two of the wine as a libation, as well).

WISE WORDS FOR LOVERS

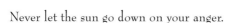

Never let the sun go down on your anger.

A good wife (or partner) and health are a man's best friend.

Love those who love you.

A woman's advice is esteemed a poor thing – but he is a fool who doesn't take it!

Discreet women have neither eyes nor ears.

Women and bees cannot be turned from their purpose.

In choosing a partner, trust not the words of another.

Love sought is good, but given unsought is better.

Faint heart never won fair maid!

You cannot give a kiss without taking, nor take without giving . . .

Don't scald your lips in another man's porridge!

Live and let love.

The longer the working, the poorer the loving!

Power can't command love, nor money buy it.

"There be none of Beauty's daughters
With a magic like thee;
And like music on the waters
Is thy sweet voice to me."
Lord Byron, *Stanzas for Music*

What is charm? It is what the violet has and
the camelia has not.
Francis Crawford, *Children of the King*

"She is not fair to outward view
As many maidens be;
Her loveliness I never knew
Until she smiled on me.
O then I saw her eye was bright,
A well of love, a spring of light."

     Hartley Coleridge, *She is not Fair*

Follow love and it will flee,
Flee love and it will follow thee.

        Anon

Love is the true price of love.

        Anon

"Love is a spirit all compact of fire,
Not gross to sink, but light, and will aspire."
William Shakespeare, *Venus and Adonis*

"Love looks not with the eyes, but with
the mind
And therefore is Wing'd Cupid painted
blind."

William Shakespeare,
A Midsummer Night's Dream

Loveliness
Needs not the foreign aid of ornament,
But is when unadorned adorned the most.

James Thomson, *The Seasons*

Do lovely things, not dream them, all day
long.

Charles Kingsley, *A Farewell*

Proverbs from around the World

(England)
Love lives in cottages as well as courts.

(Wales)
Perfect love sometimes doesn't come until the first grandchild!

(Greece)
At the touch of love, everyone becomes a prophet.

(France)
A loving heart is always young.

(Sweden)

A life without love is like a year without summer.

(Portugal)

Those who love each other tell each other a thousand things without speaking.

(China)

An old man in love is like a flower in winter.

(Japan)

A man in love mistakes a harelip for a dimple.

Acknowledgements

Many thanks to Ken Taylor for permission to use his text in the sections entitled Dream Lover, Magic Squares, and The Lesser Key of Solomon, and also for the accompanying illustrations (derived from traditional sources).